LEARNING TO READ AND WRITE

Developmentally Appropriate Practices for Young Children

Susan B. Neuman, Carol Copple, and Sue Bredekamp

A 1999 NAEYC Comprehensive Membership Benefit

National Association for the Education of Young Children—Washington, D.C.

**National Association for the Education
of Young Children**
1509 16th Street, NW
Washington, DC 20036-1426
202-232-8777 or 800-424-2460
http://www.naeyc.org

Through its publications program the National Association for the Education of Young Children (NAEYC) provides a forum for discussion of major issues and ideas in the early childhood field, with the hope of provoking thought and promoting professional growth. The views expressed or implied are not necessarily those of the Association. NAEYC thanks the authors, who donated much time and effort to develop this book as a contribution to the profession.

Library of Congress Catalog Card Number: 99-067613
ISBN 0-935989-87-0
NAEYC #161

Editor: Carol Copple; *Copyeditor:* Catherine Cauman
Editorial assistance: Debra Beland and Lacy Thompson
Design and production: Sandi Collins with Jack Zibulsky

Illustrations on pp. 37, 44, 45, 62, 68, 69, 79 (right), 87, 94, and 95: Lura Schwarz Smith

Samples of children's work were provided by the following contributors: Jeanette Amidon, Mimi Brodsky Chenfeld, Children's Village Child Care Center, Friends Community School in College Park, MD, Polly Greenberg, and Judith Schickedanz.

The authors wish to specially thank Debbie Green, director of Bright Start Child Care Center, and Mary Graham, director of Children's Village Child Care Center in Philadelphia, for allowing us to take photographs in their centers. This book includes many of their children's delightful faces engaged in developmentally appropriate literacy activities.

Printed in the United States of America.

Photo credits

p. ix: Jonathan A. Meyers; p. 20: Blakely Fetridge Bundy; p. 21: top—Larry Cumpton, bottom—Elaine M. Ward; p. 22: top & middle—Jean-Claude Lejeune, bottom—Ed Reid; p. 23: top—Jonathan A. Meyers, bottom—Cris Kelly; p. 27: Bill Geiger; p. 28: clockwise from top—Hildegard Adler, BmPorter/Don Franklin, Marilyn Nolt, Hildegard Adler; p. 29: top—Jean-Claude Lejeune, bottom left—Kent & Donna Dannen, bottom right—CLEO Photography; p. 30: Bill Geiger; p. 31: top left—Human Issues Collaborative, top right—BmPorter/Don Franklin, bottom left—Robert Settles, bottom right—Hildegard Adler; p. 32: top left—Vera Wolf/Sunrise Trinity, top right—Bill Geiger, bottom—BmPorter/Don Franklin; p. 38: top & bottom—Susan Neuman, middle—Bill Geiger; p. 39: top left—Jean-Claude Lejeune, top right—Bill Geiger, illustration courtesy of Elizabeth Jones; p. 40: top & middle—Bill Geiger, bottom—Florence Sharp; p. 41: top left—Nancy P. Alexander, top right & bottom—Jean-Claude Lejeune, middle—Bill Geiger; p. 42: top—Susan Neuman, bottom—BmPorter/Don Franklin; p. 43: top—Marietta Lynch, bottom—Jean-Claude Lejeune; p. 48: top—Bill Geiger, middle—Subjects & Predicates, bottom—Loren Fogelman; p. 49: top—Jean-Claude Lejeune, bottom—Bill Geiger; p. 50: top & middle—Jean-Claude Lejeune, bottom—Jonathan A. Meyers; p. 51: top—Jean-Claude Lejeune, middle—Bill Geiger, bottom—Elaine M. Ward; p. 52: top—Elaine M. Ward, middle—Marilyn Nolt; p. 53: top—Jonathan A. Meyers, middle right—Nancy P. Alexander, bottom—Eva Anthony; p. 56: top—Linda Werstiuk, middle—Michaelyn Straub Photography, bottom—CLEO Photography; p. 57: top—Jonathan A. Meyers, middle—Hildegard Adler, bottom—

Private Eye Photography; p. 58: top left & right—Renaud Thomas, bottom—Jonathan A. Meyers; p. 59: top & middle—Marilyn Nolt, bottom left—Sally Weigand, bottom right—Jonathan A. Meyers; p. 60: top—Jonathan A. Meyers, middle—Marietta Lynch, bottom left—Francis Wardle, bottom right—Elaine M. Ward; p. 61: top—Gail Doering, middle—Blakely Fetridge Bundy, bottom—Bill Geiger; p. 64: top—Vera Wolf/Sunrise Trinity, bottom—Larry Cumpton; p. 65: top—Bill Geiger, middle—Jean-Claude Lejeune, bottom—Ed Reid; p. 66: top—Jean-Claude Lejeune, middle—Subjects & Predicates, bottom—BmPorter/Don Franklin; p. 67: top—Jonathan A. Meyers, bottom—Jean-Claude Lejeune; p. 70: top—Bill Geiger, bottom—Nancy P. Alexander; p. 71: top & bottom—Jean-Claude Lejeune, middle—Elaine M. Ward; p. 72: top—Marietta Lynch, middle & bottom right—Bill Geiger, bottom left—BmPorter/Don Franklin; p. 73: top & bottom—Bill Geiger, middle right—Susan Klein; p. 74: top & bottom—Jean-Claude Lejeune, middle—Marietta Lynch; p. 75: top—Bill Geiger; p. 80: top—Bill Geiger, bottom—Eva Anthony; p. 81: top—Marilyn Nolt, middle & bottom—Elaine M. Ward; p. 82: top—Jean-Claude Lejeune, middle & bottom—Marilyn Nolt; p. 84: top—Renaud Thomas, middle—Marilyn Nolt, bottom—Ed Reid; p. 85: top, middle, & bottom right—Jean-Claude Lejeune, bottom left—Bill Geiger; p. 88: left—Michael Siluk, right—BmPorter/Don Franklin; p. 89: top—Bill Geiger; p. 90: top—Michael K. Smith, bottom—Jean-Claude LeJeune; p. 91: top—BmPorter/Don Franklin, bottom left and right—Bill Geiger; p. 92: both—Jean-Claude LeJeune; p. 93: top—Bill Geiger, bottom—Jean-Claude LeJeune; p. 101: Bill Geiger.

ABOUT THE AUTHORS

Susan B. Neuman is a professor in the Curriculum, Instruction and Technology in Education Department at Temple University, where she is coordinator of the Reading and Language Arts graduate program. She currently chairs the Reading and Language in Early Childhood Committee and is president of the Literacy Development for Young Children Special Interest Group for the International Reading Association (IRA). Among Dr. Neuman's publications are *Children Achieving: Best Practices in Early Literacy* (IRA), *Literacy in the Television Age* (Ablex), and *Language and Literacy in Early Childhood* (Harcourt Brace). She received her doctorate at the University of the Pacific, Stockton, California.

Carol Copple, publications editor at NAEYC, has consulted and published in the early childhood field for many years. She was on the faculty at Louisiana State University and the New School for Social Research. At the Educational Testing Service she directed the preschool laboratory program and conducted research on children's cognition. Among Dr. Copple's publications are *Educating the Young Thinker: Classroom Strategies for Cognitive Growth* (Erlbaum) and *Developmentally Appropriate Practice for Early Childhood Programs* (NAEYC). She has also written extensively for parents in magazines and newspapers. Dr. Copple received her doctorate from Cornell University.

Sue Bredekamp is currently the director of research at the Council for Early Childhood Professional Recognition and senior advisor to the Head Start Bureau. From 1984 to 1998 she served as director of professional development at NAEYC. Among the works Dr. Bredekamp has authored or coauthored are NAEYC's *Accreditation Criteria and Procedures* and *Guide to Accreditation* (three editions of each); *Developmentally Appropriate Practice in Early Childhood Programs* (NAEYC 1987; revised edition 1997) and *Reaching Potentials*, volumes 1 and 2 (NAEYC). With Susan Neuman she wrote the 1998 IRA/NAEYC joint position statement that forms the basis of this book. She holds a Ph.D. in early childhood education from the University of Maryland. Her professional experience includes teaching and directing child care and preschool programs, training child care personnel at a community college, and serving on the faculty at Mount Vernon College in Washington, D.C.

CONTENTS

PREFACE

This book is the product of a professional collaboration between early childhood educators and reading specialists, a team effort in every sense of the word. The outcome of that collaboration is better understood and appreciated if the process of its development is also known.

To begin at the beginning . . .

In January 1997 the National Association for the Education of Young Children (NAEYC) published a major revision of its bestselling book *Developmentally Appropriate Practice in Early Childhood Programs Serving Children Birth through Age 8* (Bredekamp 1987). The revised edition, *Developmentally Appropriate Practice in Early Childhood Programs* (Bredekamp & Copple 1997), came after a decade of research, debate, critique, and collaboration with many early childhood professionals and groups representing different points of view on the controversial issues that arise with respect to teaching and caring for young children.

Shortly after the revised edition was published, Jack Pikulski, then president of the International Reading Association (IRA), wrote an article responding favorably to the new edition and welcoming its changes while also raising some of the ongoing concerns about misinterpretations of developmentally appropriate practice (DAP) as meaning no teaching about literacy to young children (Pikulski 1997). Pikulski and several other IRA leaders, including Susan Neuman from Temple University, voiced concern that the revised DAP was still not explicit enough in clarifying the teacher's role in supporting early literacy development of young children, nor was the position statement sufficiently specific on the important topic of literacy (Pikulski 1997; Bredekamp 1997). Pikulski's work with kindergarten teachers convinced him that there are too many missed opportunities, and he found that DAP was often cited as the reason for not doing literacy-related activities. Neuman's research on literacy experiences in child care and Head Start programs revealed an alarming lack of books and print in the environment as well as a relative absence of teachers' explicit teaching of literacy skills and content (Neuman 1997), a concern shared by other experts in early literacy (McGill-Franzen 1993).

Under Pikulski's leadership IRA initiated a collaboration with NAEYC by appointing Sue Bredekamp, and later Carol Copple, to IRA's Committee on Reading, Language, and Early Childhood. The committee agreed that its first agenda item would be to revise the 1989 IRA position statement on early literacy that had been endorsed by NAEYC and many other organizations (IRA 1989). Beginning in May 1997, NAEYC and IRA used their conferences and Websites to solicit input from members and interested professionals.

Early on, the two groups realized that what was needed was not a revision of the earlier statement but a new position statement, because so much had been learned in the interim about both early literacy and developmentally appropriate practices. The groups agreed on several principles to guide the development of the joint position statement. The statement is thoroughly grounded in research, based on what is currently known from empirical study about early reading and writing (what we know now), and also focuses on current issues and pressing concerns about practice (the problems we are trying to fix). The statement's primary audience is teachers and teacher educators, but it is also intended for secondary audiences of parents, administrators, and policymakers. Because the statement takes a developmental view, it addresses the full age range of early childhood, from birth through 8, in terms of general principles, recommended practices, and policies. It emphasizes that it is vital to teach reading and writing to children; literacy does not just emerge naturally. Also stressed are the importance of accurate assessment of children to guide teaching and the need for responding to diversity in all its forms (individual, cultural, and linguistic).

Perhaps the most surprising but also pleasing aspect of this collaboration was the high degree of consensus among representatives of the two organizations. The surprise was probably generated by the fact that the work occurred at the height of the whole language versus phonics controversy in the United States and other parts of the English-speaking world. The media, and subsequently state and local legislators, had taken the difference of opinion within the profession as to the most effective ways to teach reading and transformed this academic debate into the Reading Wars. In the popular press most of the participants appeared to alternate between an aggressive offense and a protective defense regarding their respective positions. In this larger political context, some of us within NAEYC and IRA were justifiably wary of people whom we "knew" only through reading their opinions in journals or newspapers.

> **We now have enough knowledge to move well beyond simplistic arguments over the one right way of teaching reading.**

The more communication we had across our disciplines, however, the more we saw points of agreement. For example, what we had assumed would be the most controversial aspect of our draft position statement— articulation of the developmental continuum of early reading and writing linked to age/ grade levels—proved to be the part of the document most positively received by virtually all reviewers. The strong consensus was to include grade-connected markers of goals for children's learning because they communicate to teachers and parents that there is such a thing as a developmentally appropriate goal, while at the same time strongly emphasizing the necessity of viewing children as individuals within the continuum.

The relationships we established with colleagues, whose expertise complements but does not duplicate our own, profoundly affected the work. Reading and rereading the research, taking time to respectfully listen to each other's interpretations and points of view, using the Internet to debate and resolve differences in public e-mail conversations—these strategies and others contributed to the success of the collaboration.

We were very close to finalizing our statement in early 1998 when the National Research Council of the National Academy of Sciences released its landmark report *Preventing Reading Difficulties in Young Children* (Snow, Burns, & Griffin 1998). The Academy's procedures prohibited our having any advance knowledge of their work, so the congruity of findings and recommendations between their report and ours was doubly gratifying. It strongly signaled the end of the Reading Wars.

We now have enough knowledge to move well beyond simplistic arguments over the one right way of teaching reading and to embrace the challenges of implementing what we know in helping all children achieve their potentials as readers, writers, and communicators.

In May 1998 the boards of IRA and NAEYC each unanimously approved the joint position statement that appears in the first section of this book. But that step was only the end of the beginning. Having agreed to a course of action, the two organizations committed themselves to the goal of seeing the statement move from rhetoric to reality in the lives of young children. A logical next step was to give teachers, parents, and advocates more information and tools to achieve this goal; hence we decided to write this book.

ABOUT THIS BOOK

Our goal in producing this book is to explain the IRA/NAEYC position statement as clearly as possible—to make sense of its content for the different audiences to whom it is relevant, but especially for teachers and caregivers. The issues of how and when to teach young children to read and write are sufficiently important and controversial that our two professional associations felt the need to take an official "position." A position statement is by definition a political document, designed to address issues of controversy on which professionals can contribute knowledge and provide recommendations for practice and policy.

Only the first section of the book is the approved position statement of IRA and NAEYC. The three authors are responsible for the rest of the book, which provides elaborations and illustrations of key points of the statement with respect to instruction, assessment, and policy.

The second section, "Readers and Writers in the Making," conveys the gist of the position statement with respect to instruction, using photographs in conjunction with a summary of effective teaching practices. This section is organized into eight major themes:

- **The Power and Pleasure of Literacy**
- **The Literate Environment**
- **Language Development**
- **Building Knowledge and Comprehension**
- **Knowledge of Print**
- **Types of Text**
- **Phonological Awareness**
- **Letters and Words**

Although children's learning and development in these eight areas are closely interrelated, we see value in distinguishing these key dimensions within the child's progress towards fluent reading and writing. Also included in this section are teaching ideas that are particularly useful for development of each dimension of children's literacy learning. Finally, to help teachers consider what they are doing across all the dimensions of literacy, there is a brief self-inventory (Taking Stock of What You Do to Promote Children's Literacy).

The third section of the book, "Ensuring Children's Reading and Writing Success," consists of three parts:

- **Informing Instruction in Reading and Writing** considers assessment in this area
- **Making It Happen** outlines the policies and resources needed to support effective practice
- **Frequently Asked Questions** addresses questions that have been asked again and again in forums on reading and writing

At the back of the book we have included a glossary, a reference list, and a list of resources for teachers.

No other work is as hard as collaboration, nor is any work as ultimately rewarding. Too often collaboration is paid lip service and fails entirely. From this special collaboration between early childhood educators and reading specialists, we experienced once again the incredible power of research, respect, and relationships.

References

Bredekamp, S., ed. 1987. *Developmentally appropriate practice in programs serving children birth through age 8*. Washington, DC: NAEYC.

Bredekamp, S., & C. Copple, eds. 1997. *Developmentally appropriate practice in early childhood programs*. Rev. ed. Washington, DC: NAEYC.

International Reading Association. *Literacy development and pre-first grade*. Newark, DE: Author.

McGill-Franzen, A. 1993. "I could read the words!" Selecting good books for inexperienced readers. *The Reading Teacher* 46: 424–26.

Neuman, S.B. 1997. *Getting books in children's hands: Final report to the William Penn Foundation*. Philadelphia, PA: Temple University Press.

Pikulski, J. 1997. Reading and writing in kindergarten: Developmentally appropriate? *Reading Today* 15 (1): 24.

Snow, C.E., M.S. Burns, & P. Griffin, eds. 1998. Preventing reading difficulties in young children: Committee on the Prevention of Reading Difficulties in Young Children, Commission on Behavioral and Social Sciences and Education, National Research Council. Washington, DC: National Academy Press.

Section 1:
THE POSITION

Background
Statement of the Issues
What Research Reveals
Statement of Position

BACKGROUND

The development of this position statement began in early 1997, shortly after publication of the National Association for the Education of Young Children's revised edition of *Developmentally Appropriate Practice in Early Childhood Programs* (DAP). International Reading Association president John J. Pikulski wrote an article in *Reading Today,* IRA's bimonthly newspaper, responding favorably to the revised document and welcoming some of the changes, while also raising some ongoing concerns about misrepresentations of developmentally appropriate practice as meaning no teaching about literacy to young children. Pikulski's own work with kindergarten teachers led to his concern that there are many missed opportunities for learning in the name of developmentally appropriate practice.

IRA's Reading Language Early Childhood Committee, along with the Literacy Development in Young Children Special Interest Group, examined the new document carefully. They also expressed concern that it did not go far enough in clarifying the teacher's important role in supporting early literacy development of preschool children, and they felt that the document was not specific enough on the important topic of reading. Two subsequent articles in *Reading Today* printed critiques of the revised DAP statement. These concerns were raised at the same time that vocal arguments about reading instruction began appearing regularly in the media.

Pikulski initiated a collaboration between IRA and NAEYC by inviting Sue Bredekamp of NAEYC to serve on IRA's Reading Language Early Childhood Committee, along with Susan Neuman, who had been among the most concerned about the need to articulate developmentally appropriate practices in early literacy. The committee met for the first time at IRA's annual convention in May 1997 and agreed that the first agenda item would be to revise the 1989 IRA position statement on early literacy that had been endorsed by NAEYC and numerous other groups. The committee identified key issues to be addressed in the revised document.

Over the summer NAEYC posted the statement on its World Wide Website and requested feedback from its members. In the fall IRA set up a listserv so that NAEYC's DAP Panel and IRA'S committees, as well as other interested professionals, could discuss the issues online.

Pikulski, Bredekamp, and Neuman met in the fall of 1997 and agreed that Bredekamp and Neuman would lead the writing task and draw on the expertise of both organizations. A highly interactive two-hour open hearing was conducted at NAEYC's 1997 Annual Conference in Anaheim, California, with Pikulski, Neuman, Bredekamp, and Kathy Roskos presenting and receiving feedback from more than 300 participants. Presenters heard comments from teacher trainers, researchers, policy makers, child care staff, and parent advocates interested in children's early reading and writing development. Following the hearing, a panel from NAEYC on developmentally appropriate practice, including administrators, researchers, and U.S. Department of Education consultants, met to discuss the suggestions and agree on directions for the statement. Neuman subsequently held two open sessions with research colleagues at the National Reading Conference in early December 1997 to get their input.

The groups agreed that the statement should

1. be research based;

2. be contextualized in response to current issues or concerns about practice;

3. be addressed to a primary audience of teachers and secondary audiences of parents, administrators, and policymakers;

4. address the full age-range of birth through age eight in terms of general principles, recommended practices, and policies;

5. be reasonably brief yet long enough to support its key points;

6. address the importance of teaching, because literacy does not just emerge naturally;

7. address appropriate assessment practices;

8. be responsive to issues of cultural and linguistic diversity;

9. describe the continuum of reading and writing development and the range of individual variation; and

10. focus on reading and writing rather than on the broadest possible definition of literacy.

A thorough review of all the relevant research was conducted. In addition, every additional study that reviewers suggested for citation was read and reread. Bredekamp and Neuman wrote a draft of the position statement and circulated it for review and comment to the two committees and the Boards of Directors of NAEYC and IRA. It was also distributed for review to the members of the National Association of Early Childhood Specialists in state departments of education and to IRA's Literacy Development in Young Children Special Interest Group.

To elicit review from a still wider group of experts, NAEYC and IRA used a listserv. Although many comments were received by fax, most reviews were sent through a listserv. The level of review of this document was unprecedented as compared with the many other position statements NAEYC has developed. In fact, more than 75 thoughtful and detailed critiques were received and reviewed. Early reviews by some colleagues created a model for subsequent reviews, leading to more thorough and detailed comments than ever received previously.

Because use of a listserv ensured that the entire review process was public, the issues of controversy were debated openly and resolved through a consensus process. Every member of the group had an equal opportunity to comment. Further, this listserv was used throughout the process to summarize key discussions at meetings, highlight important points, and provide an occasional update of activities needed to finalize the document.

The position statement was revised considerably in response to the excellent reviews. The revised statement considers all the major concerns of reviewers. It needed to

1. be clearer about the role of instruction (no one naturally becomes literate, the original document lapsed into a maturation perspective at times);

2. address infants and toddlers;

3. better address bilingualism and second- language learners;

4. more thoroughly address cultural diversity;

5. better address assessment;

6. better address ongoing professional development;

7. get to the issues of controversy more succinctly;

8. address administrators; and

9. improve formatting and readability.

Some people thought the document was too long, but most felt that it needed the level of detail provided and that shorter versions could be derived from it.

The developmental continuum, which we thought might be controversial, was actually the most positively received aspect of the document. The strong consensus of reviewers was to keep the grade-connected markers of goals because they communicate to teachers that there is such a thing as a developmentally appropriate goal while emphasizing the importance of seeing children as individuals within the continuum.

The final draft of the position statement was presented for approval to the NAEYC Board of Directors at its meeting in late April 1998, and to the IRA Board of Directors in early May. It was approved unanimously by both organizations and endorsed by numerous other groups concerned with the education of young children.

The committee also outlined several additional needs to address in an expanded work plan. Among the first priorities were

1. a shortened version for teachers that could be printed in journals and placed on Websites;

2. a brochure for parents;

3. an action plan for policymakers;

4. forums (specific training at various sites) or a videoconference;

5. more detailed publications articulating the developmental continuum of reading and writing and what teachers and parents can do to support children's literacy; and

6. articles for related publications such as those of the Association for Supervision and Curriculum Development and the National Association of Elementary School Principals. The committee representatives from IRA and NAEYC have been asked to suggest implementation strategies to help achieve real change in practice and policy.

Learning to Read and Write

Developmentally Appropriate Practices for Young Children

A Joint Position Statement of
the International Reading Association (IRA) and
the National Association for the Education
of Young Children (NAEYC)
Adopted 1998

Learning to read and write is critical to a child's success in school and later in life. One of the best predictors of whether a child will function competently in school and go on to contribute actively in our increasingly literate society is the level to which the child progresses in reading and writing. Although reading and writing abilities continue to develop throughout the life span, the early childhood years—from birth through age eight—are the most important period for literacy development. It is for this reason that the International Reading Association (IRA) and the National Association for the Education of Young Children (NAEYC) joined together to formulate a position statement regarding early literacy development. The statement consists of a set of principles and recommendations for teaching practices and public policy.

The primary purpose of this position statement is to provide guidance to teachers of young children in schools and early childhood programs (including child care centers, preschools, and family child care homes) serving children from birth through age eight.

> **The early childhood years—from birth through age eight—are the most important period for literacy development.**

By and large, the principles and practices suggested here also will be of interest to any adults who are in a position to influence a young child's learning and development— parents, grandparents, older siblings, tutors, and other community members.

Teachers work in schools or programs regulated by administrative policies as well as available resources. Therefore secondary audiences for this position statement are school principals and program administrators whose roles are critical in establishing a supportive climate for sound, developmentally appropriate teaching practices, and policymakers whose decisions determine whether adequate resources are available for high-quality early childhood education.

A great deal is known about how young children learn to read and write and how they can be helped toward literacy during the first five years of life. A great deal is known also about how to help children once compulsory schooling begins, whether in kindergarten or the primary grades. Based on a thorough review of the research, this document reflects the commitment of two major professional organizations to the goal of helping children learn to read well enough by the end of third grade so that they can read to learn in all curriculum areas. IRA and NAEYC are committed not only to helping young children learn to read and write but also to fostering and sustaining their interest and disposition to read and write for their own enjoyment, information, and communication.

First, the statement summarizes the current issues that are the impetus for this position; then it reviews what is known from research on young children's literacy development. This review of research as well as the collective wisdom and experience of IRA and NAEYC members provides the basis for a position statement about what constitutes developmentally appropriate practice in early literacy over the period of birth through age eight. The position concludes with recommendations for teaching practices and policies.

STATEMENT OF THE ISSUES

Why take a position on something as obviously important as children's learning to read and write? The IRA and NAEYC believe that this position statement will contribute significantly to an improvement in practice and the development of supportive educational policies. The two associations saw that a clear, concise position statement was needed at this time for several reasons.

• It is essential and urgent to teach children to read and write competently, enabling them to achieve today's high standards of literacy.

Although the United States enjoys the highest literacy rate in its history, society now expects virtually everyone in the population to function beyond the minimum standards of literacy. Today the definition of *basic proficiency* in literacy calls for a fairly high standard of reading comprehension and analysis. The main reason is that literacy requirements of most jobs have increased significantly and are expected to increase further in the future. Communications that in the past were verbal (by phone or in person) now demand reading and writing—messages sent by electronic mail, Internet, or facsimile as well as print documents.

• With the increasing variation among young children in our programs and schools, teaching today has become more challenging.

Experienced teachers throughout the United States report that the children they teach today are more diverse in their backgrounds, experiences, and abilities than were those they taught in the past. Kindergarten classes now include children who have been in group settings for three or four years as well as children who are participating for the first time in an organized early childhood program. Classes include both children with identified disabilities and children with exceptional abilities, children who are already independent readers and children who are just beginning to acquire some basic literacy knowledge and skills. Children in the group may speak different languages at varying levels of proficiency. Because of these individual and experiential variations, it is common to find within a kindergarten classroom a five-year range in children's literacy-related skills and functioning (Riley 1996). What this means is that some kindergartners may have skills characteristic of the typical three-year-old, while others might be functioning at the level of the typical eight-year-old. Diversity is to be expected and embraced, but it can be overwhelming when teachers are expected to produce uniform outcomes for all, with no account taken of the initial range in abilities, experiences, interests, and personalities of individual children.

• Among many early childhood teachers, a maturationist view of young children's development persists despite much evidence to the contrary.

A readiness view of reading development assumes that there is a specific time in the early childhood years when the teaching of reading should begin. It also assumes that physical and neurological maturation alone prepare the child to take advantage of instruction in reading and writing. The readiness perspective implies that until children reach a certain stage of maturity all exposure to reading and writing, except perhaps being read stories, is a waste of time or even potentially harmful. Experiences throughout the early childhood years, birth through age eight, affect the development of literacy. These experiences constantly interact with characteristics of individual children to determine the level of literacy skills a child ultimately achieves. Failing to give children literacy experiences until they are in school can severely limit the reading and writing levels they ultimately attain.

• **Recognizing the early beginnings of literacy acquisition too often has resulted in use of inappropriate teaching practices suited to older children or adults perhaps but ineffective with children in preschool, kindergarten, and the early grades.**

Teaching practices associated with outdated views of literacy development and/or learning theories are still prevalent in many classrooms. Such practices include extensive whole-group instruction and intensive drill and practice on isolated skills for groups or individuals. These practices, not particularly effective for primary-grade children, are even less suitable and effective with preschool and kindergarten children. Young children especially need to be engaged in experiences that make academic content meaningful and build on prior learning. It is vital for all children to have literacy experiences in schools and early childhood programs. Such access is even more critical for children with limited home experiences in literacy. However, these school experiences must teach the broad range of language and literacy knowledge and skills to provide the solid foundation on which high levels of reading and writing ultimately depend.

Failing to give children literacy experiences until they are in school can severely limit the reading and writing levels they ultimately attain.

• **Current policies and resources are inadequate in ensuring that preschool and primary teachers are qualified to support the literacy development of all children, a task requiring strong preservice preparation and ongoing professional development.**

For teachers of children younger than kindergarten age in the United States, no uniform preparation requirements or licensure standards exist. In fact, a high school diploma is the highest level of education required to be a child care teacher in most states. Moreover, salaries in child care and preschool programs are too low to attract or retain better qualified staff. Even in the primary grades, for which certified teachers are required, many states do not offer specialized early childhood certification, which means many teachers are not adequately prepared to teach reading and writing to young children. All teachers of young children need good, foundational knowledge in language acquisition, including second-language learning, the processes of reading and writing, early literacy development, and experiences and teaching practices contributing to optimal development. Resources also are insufficient to ensure teachers continuing access to professional education so they can remain current in the field or can prepare to teach a different age group if they are reassigned.

WHAT RESEARCH REVEALS:
Rationale for the position statement

Children take their first critical steps toward learning to read and write very early in life. Long before they can exhibit reading and writing production skills, they begin to acquire some basic understandings of the concepts about literacy and its functions. Children learn to use symbols, combining their oral language, pictures, print, and play into a coherent mixed medium and creating and communicating meanings in a variety of ways. From their initial experiences and interactions with adults, children begin to read words, processing letter-sound relations and acquiring substantial knowledge of the alphabetic system. As they continue to learn, children increasingly consolidate this information into

> **Children take their first critical steps toward learning to read and write very early in life.**

patterns that allow for automaticity and fluency in reading and writing. Consequently reading and writing acquisition is better conceptualized as a developmental continuum than as an all-or-nothing phenomenon (see pp. 20–23 for "Continuum of Children's Development in Early Reading and Writing").

But the ability to read and write does not develop naturally, without careful planning and instruction. Children need regular and active interactions with print. Specific abilities required for reading and writing come from immediate experiences with oral *and* written language. Experiences in these early years begin to define the assumptions and expectations about becoming literate and give children the motivation to work toward learning to read and write. From these experiences children learn that reading and writing are valuable tools that will help them do many things in life.

The beginning years (birth through preschool)

Even in the first few months of life, children begin to experiment with language. Young babies make sounds that imitate the tones and rhythms of adult talk; they "read" gestures and facial expressions, and they begin to associate sound sequences frequently heard—words—with their referents (Berk 1996). They delight in listening to familiar jingles and rhymes, play along in games such as peekaboo and pat-a-cake, and manipulate objects such as board books and alphabet blocks in their play. From these remarkable beginnings children learn to use a variety of symbols.

In the midst of gaining facility with these symbol systems, children acquire through interactions with others the insight that specific kinds of marks—print—also can represent meanings. At first children will use the physical and visual cues surrounding print to determine what something says. But as they develop an understanding of the alphabetic principle, children begin to process letters, translate them into sounds,

and connect this information with a known meaning. Although it may seem as though some children acquire these understandings magically or on their own, studies suggest that they are the beneficiaries of considerable, though playful and informal, adult guidance and instruction (Durkin 1966; Anbar 1986).

Considerable diversity in children's oral and written language experiences occurs in these years (Hart & Risley 1995). In home and child care situations, children encounter many different resources and types and degrees of support for early reading and writing (McGill-Franzen & Lanford 1994). Some children may have ready access to a range of writing and reading materials, while others may not; some children will observe their parents writing and reading frequently, others only occasionally; some children receive direct instruction, while others receive much more casual, informal assistance.

> **Reading and writing acquisition is better conceptualized as a developmental continuum than as an all-or-nothing phenomenon.**

What this means is that no one teaching method or approach is likely to be the most effective for all children (Strickland 1994). Rather, good teachers bring into play a variety of teaching strategies that can encompass the great diversity of children in schools. Excellent instruction builds on what children already know, and can do, and provides knowledge, skills, and dispositions for lifelong learning. Children need to learn not only the technical skills of reading and writing but also how to use these tools to better their thinking and reasoning (Neuman 1998).

The single most important activity for building these understandings and skills essential for reading success appears to be *reading aloud to children* (Wells 1985; Bus, van IJzendoorn, & Pellegrini 1995). High-quality book reading occurs when children feel emotionally secure (Bus & van IJzendoorn 1995; Bus et al. 1997) and are active participants in reading (Whitehurst et al. 1994). Asking predictive and analytic questions in small-group settings appears to affect children's vocabulary and comprehension of stories (Karweit & Wasik 1996). Children may talk about the pictures, retell the story, discuss their favorite actions, and request multiple rereadings. It is the talk that surrounds the storybook reading that gives it power, helping children to bridge what is in the story and their own lives (Dickinson & Smith 1994; Snow et al. 1995). Snow (1991) has described these types of conversations as "decontextualized language" in which teachers may induce higher-level thinking by moving experiences in stories from what the children may see in front of them to what they can imagine.

A central goal during these preschool years is to enhance children's *exposure to and concepts about print* (Clay 1979, 1991; Holdaway 1979; Teale 1984; Stanovich & West 1989). Some teachers use Big Books to help children distinguish many print features, including the fact that print (rather than pictures) carries the meaning of the story, that the strings of letters between spaces are words and in print correspond to an oral version, and that reading progresses from left to right and top to bottom. In the course of reading stories, teachers may demonstrate these features by pointing to individual words, directing children's attention to where to begin reading, and helping children to recognize letter shapes and sounds. Some researchers (Adams 1990; Roberts 1998) have suggested that the key to these critical concepts, such as developing word awareness, may lie in these demonstrations of how print works.

Children also need opportunity to practice what they've learned about print with their peers and on their own. Studies suggest that the physical arrangement of the classroom can promote time with books (Morrow & Weinstein 1986; Neuman & Roskos 1997). A key area is the classroom library—a collection of attractive stories and informational books that provides children with immediate access to books. Regular visits to the school

> **No one teaching method or approach is likely to be the most effective for all children. Rather, good teachers bring into play a variety of teaching strategies that can encompass the great diversity of children in schools.**

or public library and library card registration ensure that children's collections remain continually updated and may help children develop the habit of reading as lifelong learning. In comfortable library settings children often will pretend to read, using visual cues to remember the words of their favorite stories. Although studies have shown that these pretend readings are just that (Ehri & Sweet 1991), such visual readings may demonstrate substantial knowledge about the global features of reading and its purposes.

Storybooks are not the only means of providing children with exposure to written language. Children learn a lot about reading from the labels, signs, and other kinds of print they see around them (McGee, Lomax, & Head 1988; Neuman & Roskos 1993). Highly visible print labels on objects, signs, and bulletin boards in classrooms demonstrate the practical uses of written language. In environments rich with print, children incorporate literacy into their dramatic play (Morrow 1990; Vukelich 1994; Neuman & Roskos 1997), using these communication tools to enhance the drama and realism of the pretend situation. These everyday, playful experiences by themselves do not make most children readers. Rather, they expose children to a variety of print experiences and the processes of reading for real purposes.

For children whose primary language is other than English, studies have shown that a strong basis in a first language promotes school achievement in a second language (Cummins 1979). Children who are *learning English as a second language* are more likely to become readers and writers of English when they are already familiar with the vocabulary and concepts in their primary language. In this respect, oral and

> **The ability to read and write does not develop naturally, without careful planning and instruction.**

> **The single most important activity for building these understandings and skills essential for reading success appears to be reading aloud to children.**

written language experiences should be regarded as an additive process, ensuring that children are able to maintain their home language while also learning to speak and read English (Wong Fillmore 1991). Including non-English materials and resources to the extent possible can help to support children's first language while children acquire oral proficiency in English.

A fundamental insight developed in children's early years through instruction is the *alphabetic principle,* the understanding that there is a systematic relationship between letters and sounds (Adams 1990). The research of Gibson and Levin (1975) indicates that the shapes of letters are learned by distinguishing one character from another by its type of spatial features. Teachers will often involve children in comparing letter shapes, helping them to differentiate a number of letters visually. Alphabet books and alphabet puzzles in which children can see and compare letters may be a key to efficient and easy learning.

At the same time, children learn about the sounds of language through exposure to *linguistic awareness* games, nursery rhymes, and rhythmic activities. Some research suggests that the roots of phonemic awareness, a powerful predictor of later reading success, are found in traditional rhyming, skipping, and word games (Bryant et al. 1990). In one study (Maclean, Bryant, & Bradley 1987), for example, researchers found that three-year-old children's knowledge of nursery rhymes specifically related to their more abstract phonological knowledge later on. Engaging children in choral readings of rhymes and rhythms allows them to associate the symbols with the sounds they hear in these words.

Although children's facility in phonemic awareness has been shown to be strongly related to later reading achievement, the precise role it plays in these early years is not fully understood. *Phonemic awareness* refers to a child's understanding and conscious awareness that speech is composed of identifiable units, such as spoken words, syllables, and sounds. Training studies have demonstrated that phonemic awareness can be taught to children as young as age five (Bradley & Bryant 1983; Lundberg, Frost, & Petersen 1988; Cunningham 1990; Bryne & Fielding-Barnsley 1991). These studies used tiles (boxes) (Elkonin 1973) and linguistic games to engage children in explicitly manipulating speech segments at the phoneme level. Yet, whether such training is appropriate for younger children is highly suspect. Other scholars find that children benefit most from such training only after they have learned some letter names, shapes, and sounds and can apply what they learn to real reading in meaningful contexts (Cunningham 1990; Foorman et al. 1991). Even at this later age, however, many children acquire phonemic awareness skills without specific training but as a consequence of learning to read (Wagner & Torgesen 1987; Ehri 1994). In the preschool years sensitizing children to sound similarities does not seem to be strongly dependent on formal training but rather from listening to patterned, predictable texts while enjoying the feel of reading and language.

Children acquire a working knowledge of the alphabetic system not only through reading but also through writing. A classic study by Read (1971) found that even without formal spelling instruction, preschoolers use their tacit knowledge of phonological relations to spell words. *Invented spelling* (or *phonic spelling*) refers to beginners' use of the symbols they associate with the sounds they hear in the words they wish to write. For example, a child may initially write *b* or *bk* for the word *bike,* to be followed by more conventionalized forms later on.

> **In environments rich with print, children incorporate literacy into their dramatic play, using these tools to enhance the drama and realism of the pretend situation.**

Some educators may wonder whether invented spelling promotes poor spelling habits. To the contrary, studies suggest that *temporary* invented spelling may contribute to beginning reading (Chomsky 1979; Clarke 1988). One study, for example, found that children benefited from using invented spelling compared to having the teacher provide correct spellings in writing (Clarke 1988). Although children's invented spellings did not comply with correct spellings, the process encouraged them to think actively about letter-sound relations. As children engage in writing, they are learning to segment the words they wish to spell into constituent sounds.

> **The roots of phonemic awareness, which is related to later reading success, are found in traditional rhyming, skipping, and word games.**

Classrooms that provide children with regular opportunities to express themselves on paper, without feeling too constrained for correct spelling and proper handwriting, also help children understand that writing has real purpose (Graves 1983; Sulzby 1985; Dyson 1988). Teachers can organize situations that both demonstrate the writing process and get children actively involved in it. Some teachers serve as scribes and help children write down their ideas, keeping in mind the balance between children doing it themselves and asking for help. In the beginning these products likely emphasize pictures with few attempts at writing letters or words. With encouragement, children begin to label their pictures, tell stories, and attempt to write stories about the pictures they have drawn. Such novice writing activity sends the important message that writing is not just handwriting practice—children are using their own words to compose a message to communicate with others.

Thus the picture that emerges from research in these first years of children's reading and writing is one that emphasizes wide exposure to print and to developing concepts about it and its forms and functions. Classrooms filled with print, language and literacy play, storybook reading, and writing allow children to experience the joy and power associated with reading and writing while mastering basic concepts about print that research has shown are strong predictors of achievement.

In kindergarten

Knowledge of the forms and functions of print serves as a foundation from which children become increasingly sensitive to letter shapes, names, sounds, and words. However, not all children typically come to kindergarten with similar levels of knowledge about printed language. Estimating where each child is developmentally and building on that base, a key feature of all good teaching, is particularly important for the kindergarten teacher. Instruction will need to be adapted to account for children's differences. For those children with lots of print experiences, instruction will extend their knowledge as they learn more about the formal features of letters and their sound correspondences. For other children with fewer prior experiences, initiating them to the alphabetic principle, that the alphabet comprises a limited set of letters and that these letters stand for the sounds that make up spoken words, will require more focused and direct instruction. In all cases, however, children need to interact with a rich variety of print (Morrow, Strickland, & Woo 1998).

In this critical year kindergarten teachers need to capitalize on every opportunity for enhancing children's *vocabulary development.* One approach is through listening to stories (Feitelson, Kita, &

> **Children acquire a working knowledge of the alphabetic system not only through reading but also through writing. Their efforts to spell encourage them to think actively about letter-sound relations.**

Goldstein 1986; Elley 1989). Children need to be exposed to vocabulary from a wide variety of genres, including informational texts as well as narratives. The learning of vocabulary, however, is not necessarily simply a byproduct of reading stories (Leung & Pikulski 1990). Some explanation of vocabulary words prior to listening to a story is related significantly to children's learning of new words (Elley 1989). Dickinson and Smith (1994), for example, found that asking predictive and analytic questions before and after the readings produced positive effects on vocabulary and comprehension.

Repeated readings appear to further reinforce the language of the text as well as to familiarize children with the way different genres are structured (Eller, Pappas, & Brown 1988; Morrow 1988). Understanding the forms of informational and narrative texts seems to distinguish those children who have been well read to from those who have not (Pappas 1991). In one study, for example, Pappas found that with multiple exposures to a story (three readings), children's retelling became increasingly rich, integrating what they knew about the world, the language of the book, and the message of the author. Thus, considering the benefits for vocabulary development and comprehension, the case is strong for interactive storybook reading (Anderson 1995). Increasing the volume of children's playful, stimulating experiences with good books is associated with accelerated growth in reading competence.

Activities that help children clarify the *concept of word* are also worthy of time and attention in the kindergarten curriculum (Juel 1991). Language experience charts that let teachers demonstrate how talk can be written down provide a natural medium for children's developing word awareness in meaningful contexts. Transposing children's spoken words into written symbols through

> **Estimating where each child is developmentally and building on that base, a key feature of all good teaching, is particularly important for the kindergarten teacher.**

> **Teachers need to capitalize on every opportunity for enhancing children's vocabulary development.**

dictation provides a concrete demonstration that strings of letters between spaces are words and that not all words are the same length. Studies by Clay (1979) and Bissex (1980) confirm the value of what many teachers have known and done for years: Teacher dictations of children's stories help develop word awareness, spelling, and the conventions of written language.

Many children enter kindergarten with at least some perfunctory knowledge of the alphabet letters. An important goal for the kindergarten teacher is to reinforce this skill by ensuring that children can recognize and discriminate these letter shapes with increasing ease and fluency (Mason 1980; Snow, Burns, & Griffin 1998). Children's proficiency in *letter naming* is a well-established predictor of their end-of-year achievement (Bond & Dykstra 1967; Riley 1996), probably because it mediates the ability to remember sounds. Generally a good rule according to current learning theory (Adams 1990) is to start with the more easily visualized uppercase letters, to be followed by identifying lowercase letters. In each case, introducing just a few letters at a time, rather than many, enhances mastery.

At about the time children are readily able to identify letter names, they begin to connect the letters with the sounds they hear. A fundamental insight in this phase of learning is that a letter and letter sequences map onto phonological forms. Phonemic awareness, however, is not merely a solitary insight or an instant ability (Juel 1991). It takes time and practice.

Children who are phonemically aware can think about and manipulate sounds in words. They know when words rhyme or do not; they know when words begin or end with the same sound; and they know that a word like *bat* is composed of three sounds /b/ /a/ /t/ and that these sounds can be blended into a spoken word. Popular rhyming books, for example, may draw children's attention to rhyming patterns, serving as a basis for extending vocabulary (Ehri & Robbins 1992). Using initial letter cues, children can learn many new words through analogy, taking the familiar word *bake* as a strategy for figuring out a new word, *lake.*

Further, as teachers engage children in shared writing, they can pause before writing a word, say it slowly, and stretch out the sounds as they write it. Such activities in the context of real reading and writing help children attend to the features of print and the alphabetic nature of English.

There is accumulated evidence that instructing children in phonemic awareness activities in kindergarten (and first grade) enhances reading achievement (Stanovich 1986; Lundberg, Frost, & Petersen 1988; Bryne & Fielding-Barnsley 1991, 1993, 1995). Although a large number of children will acquire phonemic awareness skills as they learn to read, an estimated 20% will not without additional training. A statement by the IRA (1998) indicates that "the likelihood of these students becoming successful as readers is slim to none. . . . This figure [20%], however, can be substantially reduced through more systematic attention to engagement with language early on in the child's home, preschool and kindergarten classes." A study by Hanson and Farrell (1995), for example, examined the long-term benefits of a carefully developed kindergarten curriculum that focused on word study and decoding skills, along with sets of stories so that children would be able to practice these skills in meaningful contexts. High school seniors who early on had received this type of instruction outperformed their counterparts on reading achievement, attitude toward schooling, grades, and attendance.

In kindergarten many children will begin to read some words through recognition or by processing letter-sound relations. Studies by Domico (1993) and Richgels (1995) suggest that children's ability to read words is tied to their ability to write words in a somewhat reciprocal relationship. The more opportunities children have to

> **Children's profiency in letter naming is a well-established predictor of their achievement at the end of kindergarten.**

> **Effective instruction includes rich demonstrations, interactions, and models of literacy in the course of activities that make sense to young children.**

write, the greater the likelihood that they will reproduce spellings of words they have seen and heard. Though not conventional, these spellings likely show greater letter-sound correspondences and partial encoding of some parts of words, like *SWM* for *swim,* than do the inventions of preschoolers (Clay 1975).

To provide more intensive and extensive practice, some teachers try to integrate writing in other areas of the curriculum, like literacy-related play (Neuman & Roskos 1992), and other project activities (Katz & Chard 1989). These types of projects engage children in using reading and writing for multiple purposes while they are learning about topics meaningful to them.

Early literacy activities teach children a great deal about writing and reading but often in ways that do not look much like traditional elementary school instruction. Capitalizing on the active and social nature of children's learning, early instruction must provide rich demonstrations, interactions, and models of literacy in the course of activities that make sense to young children. Children must also learn about the relation between oral and written language and the relation between letters, sounds, and words. In classrooms built around a wide variety of print activities and in talking, reading, writing, playing, and listening to one another, children will want to read and write and feel capable that they can do so.

The primary grades

Instruction takes on a more formal nature as children move into the elementary grades. Here it is virtually certain that children will receive at least some instruction from a commercially published product, like a basal or literature anthology series.

Although research has clearly established that no one method is superior for all children (Bond & Dykstra 1967; Snow, Burns, & Griffin 1998), approaches that favor some type of *systematic code instruction along with meaningful connected reading* report children's superior progress in reading. Instruction should aim to teach the important letter-sound relationships, which once learned are practiced through having many opportunities to read. Most likely these research findings are a positive result of the Matthew Effect, the rich-get-richer effects that are embedded in such instruction; that is, children who acquire alphabetic coding skills begin to recognize many words (Stanovich 1986). As word recognition processes become more automatic, children are likely to allocate more attention to higher-level processes of comprehension. Since these reading experiences tend to be rewarding for children, they may read more often; thus reading achievement may be a byproduct of reading enjoyment.

One of the hallmarks of skilled reading is *fluent, accurate word identification* (Juel, Griffith, & Gough 1986). Yet instruction in simply word calling with flashcards is not reading. Real reading is comprehension. Children need to read a wide variety of interesting, comprehensible materials, which they can read orally with about 90 to 95% accuracy (Durrell & Catterson 1980). In the beginning children are likely to read slowly and deliberately as they focus on exactly what's on the page. In fact they may seem "glued to print" (Chall 1983), figuring out the fine points of form at the word level. However, children's reading expression, fluency, and comprehension generally improve when they read familiar texts. Some authorities have found the practice of repeated rereadings in which

> **In the primary grades, approaches that favor some type of systematic code instruction along with meaningful connected reading promote children's superior progress in reading.**

> **Real reading is comprehension.**

children reread short selections significantly enhances their confidence, fluency, and comprehension in reading (Samuels 1979; Moyer 1982).

Children not only use their increasing knowledge of letter-sound patterns to read unfamiliar texts. They also use a variety of strategies. Studies reveal that early readers are capable of being intentional in their use of *metacognitive strategies* (Brown & DeLoache 1978; Rowe 1994) Even in these early grades, children make predictions about what they are to read, self-correct, reread, and question if necessary, giving evidence that they are able to adjust their reading when understanding breaks down. Teacher practices, such as the Directed Reading-Thinking Activity (DRTA), effectively model these strategies by helping children set purposes for reading, ask questions, and summarize ideas through the text (Stauffer 1970).

But children also need time for *independent practice.* These activities may take on numerous forms. Some research, for example, has demonstrated the powerful effects that children's reading to their caregivers has on promoting confidence as well as reading proficiency (Hannon 1995). Visiting the library and scheduling independent reading and writing periods in literacy-rich classrooms also provide children with opportunities to select books of their own choosing. They may engage in the social activities of reading with their peers, asking questions, and writing stories (Morrow & Weinstein 1986), all of which may nurture interest and appreciation for reading and writing.

Supportive relationships between these communication processes lead many teachers to *integrate reading and writing* in classroom instruction (Tierney & Shanahan 1991). After all, writing challenges children to actively think about print. As young authors struggle to express themselves, they come to grips with different written forms, syntactic patterns, and themes. They use writing for multiple purposes: to write descriptions, lists, and stories to communicate with others. It is important for teachers to expose children to a range of text forms, including stories, reports, and informational texts, and to help children select vocabulary and punctuate simple sentences that meet the demands of audience and purpose. Since handwriting instruction helps children communicate effectively, it should also be part of the writing process (McGee & Richgels 1996). Short lessons demonstrating certain letter formations tied to the publication of writing provide an ideal time for instruction. Reading and writing workshops, in which teachers provide small-group and individual instruction, may help children to develop the skills they need for communicating with others.

Although children's initial writing drafts will contain invented spellings, learning about spelling will take on increasing importance in these years (Henderson & Beers 1980; Richgels 1986). *Spelling instruction* should be an important component of the reading and writing program since it directly affects reading ability. Some teachers create their own spelling lists, focusing on words with common patterns and high-frequency words, as well as some personally meaningful words from the children's writing. Research indicates that seeing a word in print, imagining how it is spelled, and copying new words is an effective way of acquiring spellings (Barron 1980). Nevertheless, even though the teacher's goal is to foster more conventionalized forms, it is important to recognize that there is more to writing than just spelling and grammatically correct sentences. Rather, writing has been characterized by Applebee (1977) as "thinking with a pencil." It is true that children will need adult help to master the complexities of the writing process. But they also will need to learn that the power of writing is expressing one's own ideas in ways that can be understood by others.

As children's capabilities develop and become more fluent, instruction will turn from a central focus on helping children learn to read and write to helping them read and write to learn. Increasingly the emphasis for teachers will be on encouraging children to become *independent and productive readers,* helping them to extend their reasoning and comprehension abilities in learning about their world. Teachers will need to provide challenging materials that require children to analyze and think creatively and from different points of view. They also will need to ensure that children have practice in reading and writing (both in and out of school) and many opportunities to

> **Accurate assessment of children's knowledge, skills, and dispositions in reading and writing will help teachers better match instruction with how and what children are learning.**

analyze topics, generate questions, and organize written responses for different purposes in meaningful activities.

Throughout these critical years *accurate assessment* of children's knowledge, skills, and dispositions in reading and writing will help teachers better match instruction with how and what children are learning. However, early reading and writing cannot simply be measured as a set of narrowly-defined skills on standardized tests. These measures often are not reliable or valid indicators of what children can do in typical practice, nor are they sensitive to language variation, culture, or the experiences of young children (Shepard & Smith 1988; Shepard 1994; Johnston 1997). Rather, a sound assessment should be anchored in real-life writing and reading tasks and continuously chronicle a wide range of children's literacy activities in different situations. Good assessment is essential to help teachers tailor appropriate instruction to young children and to know when and how much intensive instruction on any particular skill or strategy might be needed.

By the end of third grade, children will still have much to learn about literacy. Clearly some will be further along the path to independent reading and writing than others. Yet with high-quality instruction, the majority of children will be able to decode words with a fair degree of facility, use a variety of strategies to adapt to different types of text, and be able to communicate effectively for multiple purposes using conventionalized spelling and punctuation. Most of all they will have come to see themselves as capable readers and writers, having mastered the complex set of attitudes, expectations, behaviors, and skills related to written language.

STATEMENT OF POSITION

IRA and NAEYC believe that achieving high standards of literacy for every child in the United States is a shared responsibility of schools, early childhood programs, families, and communities. But teachers of young children, whether employed in preschools, child care programs, or elementary schools, have a unique responsibility to promote children's literacy development, based on the most current professional knowledge and research.

A review of research along with the collective wisdom and experience of members has led IRA and NAEYC to conclude that learning to read and write is a complex, multifaceted process that requires a wide variety of instructional approaches, a conclusion similar to that reached by an esteemed panel of experts for the National Academy of Sciences (Snow, Burns, & Griffin 1998).

Similarly, this review of research leads to a theoretical model of literacy learning and development as an interactive process. Research supports the view of the child as an active constructor of his or her own learning, while at the same time studies emphasize the critical role of the supportive, interested, engaged adult (e.g., teacher, parent, or tutor) who provides scaffolding for the child's development of greater skill and understanding (Mason & Sinha 1993; Riley 1996). The principle of learning is that "children are active learners, drawing on direct social and physical experience as well as culturally transmitted knowledge to construct their own understandings of the world around them" (Bredekamp & Copple 1997, 13).

IRA and NAEYC believe that goals and expectations for young children's achievement in reading and

> **As children move toward third grade and beyond, teachers will place increasing emphasis on helping them to become independent and productive readers—that is, on reading to learn.**

> **Learning to read and write is a complex, multifaceted process that requires a wide variety of instructional approaches.**

writing should be developmentally appropriate, that is, *challenging but achievable,* with sufficient adult support. A continuum of reading and writing development is generally accepted and useful for teachers in understanding the goals of literacy instruction and in assessing children's progress toward those goals. (An abbreviated continuum of reading and writing development appears on pp. 20–23; for more detailed examples, see Chall 1983; Education Department of Western Australia 1994; Whitmore & Goodman 1995; Snow, Burns, & Griffin 1998). Good teachers understand that children do not progress along this developmental continuum in rigid sequence. Rather, each child exhibits a unique pattern and timing in acquiring skills and understanding related to reading and writing.

Like other complex skills, reading and writing are outcomes that result from the continual interplay of development and learning, and therefore a range of individual variation is to be expected in the rate and pace at which children gain literacy skills. Given exposure to appropriate literacy experiences and good teaching during early childhood, most children learn to read at age six or seven, a few learn at four, some learn at five, and others need intensive individualized support to learn to read at eight or nine. Some children who do not explore books and other print during their early years are likely to need more focused support for literacy development when they enter an educational program, whether at preschool, kindergarten, or first grade (since preschool and even kindergarten attendance is not universal). Other children who enter school speaking little or no English are likely to need instructional strategies in their home language (Snow, Burns, & Griffin 1998).

Given the range within which children typically master reading, even with exposure to print-rich environments and good teaching, a developmentally appropriate expectation is for most children to achieve beginning conventional reading (also called early reading) by age seven. For children with disabilities or special learning needs, achievable but challenging goals for their individual reading and writing development in an inclusive environment are established by teachers, families, and specialists working in collaboration (DEC Task Force 1993; DEC/CEC 1994).

IRA and NAEYC believe that early childhood teachers need to understand the developmental continuum of reading and writing and be skilled in a variety of strategies to assess and support individual children's development and learning across the continuum. At the same time teachers must set developmentally appropriate literacy goals for young children and then adapt instructional strategies for children whose learning and development are advanced or lag behind those goals. Good teachers make instructional decisions based on their knowledge of reading and writing, current research, appropriate expectations, and their knowledge of individual children's strengths and needs.

A continuum of reading and writing development is useful for identifying challenging but achievable goals or benchmarks for children's literacy learning, remembering that individual variation is to be expected and supported. Using a developmental continuum enables teachers to assess individual children's progress against realistic goals and then adapt instruction to ensure that children continue to progress. During the preschool years most children can be expected to function in phase 1 of the developmental continuum, Awareness and Exploration. In kindergarten an appropriate expectation is that most children will be at phase 2, Experimental Reading and Writing. By the end of first grade, most children will

> **Familiarity with the developmental continuum enables teachers to assess individual children's progress against realistic goals and then adapt instruction to ensure that children continue to progress.**

> **Goals and expectations for young children's achievement in reading and writing should be developmentally appropriate, that is, *challenging but achievable,* with sufficient adult support.**

function in phase 3, Early Reading and Writing. An appropriate expectation for second grade is Transitional Reading and Writing (phase 4), while the goal for third grade is Independent and Productive Reading and Writing (phase 5). Advanced Reading is the goal for fourth grade and above.

As fundamental as the principle of individual variation is the principle that human development and learning occur in and are influenced by social and cultural contexts. Language, reading, and writing are strongly shaped by culture. Children enter early childhood programs or schools having learned to communicate and make sense of their experiences at home and in their communities. When the ways of making and communicating meaning are similar at home and in school, children's transitions are eased. However, when the language and culture of the home and school are not congruent, teachers and parents must work together to help children strengthen and preserve their home language and culture while acquiring skills needed to participate in the shared culture of the school (NAEYC 1996a).

Most important, teachers must understand how children learn a second language and how this process applies to young children's literacy development. Teachers need to respect the child's home language and culture and use it as a base on which to build and extend children's language and literacy experiences. Unfortunately teachers too often react negatively to children's linguistic and cultural diversity, equating difference with deficit. Such situations hurt children whose abilities within their own cultural context are not recognized because they do not match the cultural expectations of the school. Failing to recognize children's strengths or capabilities, teachers may underestimate their competence. Competence is not tied to any particular language, dialect, or culture. Teachers should never use a child's dialect, language, or culture as a basis for making judgments about the child's intellect or capability. Linguistically and culturally diverse children bring multiple perspectives and impressive skills, such as code-switching (the ability to go back and forth between two languages to deepen conceptual understanding), to the tasks of learning to speak, read, and write a second language. These self-motivated, self-initiating, constructive thinking processes should be celebrated and used as rich teaching and learning resources for all children.

RECOMMENDED TEACHING PRACTICES

During the infant and toddler years. Children need relationships with caring adults who engage in many one-on-one, face-to-face interactions with them to support their oral language development and lay the foundation for later literacy learning. Important experiences and teaching behaviors include but are not limited to

• talking to babies and toddlers with simple language, frequent eye contact, and responsiveness to children's cues and language attempts;

• frequently playing with, talking to, singing to, and doing fingerplays with very young children;

• sharing cardboard books with babies and frequently reading to toddlers on the adult's lap or together with one or two other children; and

• providing simple art materials such as crayons, markers, and large paper for toddlers to explore and manipulate.

During the preschool years. Young children need developmentally appropriate experiences and teaching to support literacy learning. These include but are not limited to

• positive, nurturing relationships with adults who engage in responsive conversations with individual children, model reading and writing behavior, and foster children's interest in and enjoyment of reading and writing;

> **Competence is not tied to any particular language, dialect, or culture. Teachers should never use a child's dialect, language, or culture as a basis for making judgments about the child's intellect or capability.**

• print-rich environments that provide opportunities and tools for children to see and use written language for a variety of purposes, with teachers drawing children's attention to specific letters and words;

• adults' daily reading of high-quality books to individual children or small groups, including books that positively reflect children's identity, home language, and culture;

• opportunities for children to talk about what is read and to focus on the sounds and parts of language as well as the meaning;

• teaching strategies and experiences that develop phonemic awareness, such as songs, fingerplays, games, poems, and stories in which phonemic patterns such as rhyme and alliteration are salient;

• opportunities to engage in play that incorporates literacy tools, such as writing grocery lists in dramatic play, making signs in block building, and using icons and words in exploring a computer game; and

• firsthand experiences that expand children's vocabulary, such as trips in the community and exposure to various tools, objects, and materials.

In kindergarten and primary grades. Teachers should continue many of these same good practices with the goal of continually advancing children's learning and development (see the "Continuum of Children's Development in Early Reading and Writing" on pp.20–23 for appropriate grade-level expectations). In addition every child is entitled to excellent instruction in reading and writing that includes but is not limited to

• daily experiences of being read to and independently reading meaningful and engaging stories and informational texts;

• a balanced instructional program that includes systematic code instruction along with meaningful reading and writing activities;

• daily opportunities and teacher support to write many kinds of texts for different purposes, including stories, lists, messages to others, poems, reports, and responses to literature;

• writing experiences that allow the flexibility to use nonconventional forms of writing at first (invented or phonic spelling) and over time move to conventional forms;

• opportunities to work in small groups for focused instruction and collaboration with other children;

• an intellectually engaging and challenging curriculum that expands knowledge of the world and vocabulary; and

• adaptation of instructional strategies or more individualized instruction if the child fails to make expected progress in reading or when literacy skills are advanced.

Although experiences during the earliest years of life can have powerful long-term consequences, human beings are amazingly resilient and incredibly capable of learning throughout life. We should strengthen our resolve to ensure that every child has the benefit of positive early childhood experiences that support literacy development. At the same time, regardless of children's prior learning, schools have the responsibility to educate every child and to never give up even if later interventions must be more intensive and costly.

> **During the infant and toddler years, children need relationships with caring adults who engage in many one-on-one, face-to-face interactions with them to support their oral language development and lay the foundation for later literacy learning.**

> **We should ensure that every child has the positive early childhood experiences that support literacy development. At the same time, regardless of children's prior learning, schools have the responsibility to educate every child and never give up even if later interventions must be more intensive and costly.**

RECOMMENDED POLICIES ESSENTIAL FOR ACHIEVING DEVELOPMENTALLY APPROPRIATE LITERACY EXPERIENCES

Early childhood programs and elementary schools in the United States operate in widely differing contexts with varying levels of funding and resources. Regardless of the resources available, professionals have an ethical responsibility to teach, to the best of their ability, according to the standards of the profession. Nevertheless, the kinds of practices advocated here are more likely to be implemented within an infrastructure of supportive policies and resources. IRA and NAEYC strongly recommend that the following policies be developed and adequately funded at the appropriate state or local levels:

1. A comprehensive, consistent system of early childhood professional preparation and ongoing professional development (see Darling-Hammond 1997; Kagan & Cohen 1997).

Such a professional preparation system is badly needed in every state to ensure that staff in early childhood programs and teachers in primary schools obtain specialized, college-level education that informs them about developmental patterns in early literacy learning and about research-based ways of teaching reading and writing during the early childhood years. Ongoing professional de-

> **Ongoing professional development is essential for teachers to stay current in an ever-expanding research base and to continually improve their teaching skills and the learning outcomes for children.**

velopment is essential for teachers to stay current in an ever-expanding research base and to continually improve their teaching skills and the learning outcomes for children.

2. Sufficient resources to ensure adequate ratios of qualified teachers to children and small groups for individualizing instruction.

For four- and five-year-olds, adult-child ratios should be 1 adult for no more than 8 to 10 children, with a maximum group size of 20 (Howes, Phillips, & Whitebook 1992; Cost, Quality, and Child Outcomes Study Team 1995). Optimum class size in the early grades is 15 to 18 with one teacher (Nye et al. 1992; Nye, Boyd-Zaharias, & Fulton 1994). Young children benefit most from being taught in small groups or as individuals. There will always be a wide range of individual differences among children. Small class size increases the likelihood that teachers will be able to accommodate children's diverse abilities and interests, strengths and needs.

3. Sufficient resources to ensure classrooms, schools, and public libraries that include a wide range of high-quality children's books, computer software, and multimedia resources at various levels of difficulty and reflecting various cultural and family backgrounds.

Studies have found that a minimum of five books per child is necessary to provide even the most basic print-rich environment (Morrow & Weinstein 1986; Neuman & Roskos 1997). Computers and developmentally appropriate software should also be avail-

able to provide alternative, engaging, enriching literacy experiences (NAEYC 1996b).

4. Policies that promote children's continuous learning progress.

When individual children do not make expected progress in literacy development, resources should be available to provide more individualized instruction, focused time, tutoring by trained and qualified tutors, or other individualized intervention strategies. These instructional strategies are used to accelerate children's learning instead of either grade retention or social promotion, neither of which has been proven effective in improving children's achievement (Shepard & Smith 1988).

5. Appropriate assessment strategies that promote children's learning and development.

Teachers need to regularly and systematically use multiple indicators—observation of children's oral language, evaluation of children's work, and performance at authentic reading and writing tasks—to assess and monitor children's progress in reading and writing development, plan and adapt instruction, and communicate with parents (Shepard, Kagan, & Wurtz 1998). Group-administered, multiple-choice standardized achievement tests in reading and writing skills should not be used before third grade or preferably even before fourth grade. The younger the child, the more difficult it is to obtain valid and reliable indices of his or her development and learning using one-time test administrations. Standardized testing has a legitimate function, but on its own it tends to lead to standardized teaching—one approach fits all—the opposite of the kind of individualized diagnosis and teaching that is needed to help young children continue to progress in reading and writing.

6. Access to regular, ongoing health care for every child.

Every young child needs to have a regular health care provider as well as screening for early diagnosis and treatment of vision and hearing problems. Chronic untreated middle-ear infections in the earliest years of life may delay language development, which in turn may delay reading development (Vernon-Feagans, Emanuel, & Blood 1992). Similarly, vision problems should never be allowed to go uncorrected, causing a child difficulty with reading and writing.

7. Increased public investment to ensure access to high-quality preschool and child care programs for all children who need them.

The National Academy of Sciences (Snow, Burns, & Griffin 1998) and decades of longitudinal research (see, for example, Barnett 1995) demonstrate the benefits of preschool education for literacy learning. Unfortunately, there is no system to ensure accessible, affordable, high-quality early childhood education programs for all families who choose to use them (Kagan & Cohen 1997). As a result, preschool attendance varies considerably by family income; for example, 80% of four-year-olds whose families earn more than U.S. $50,000 per year attend preschool compared to approximately 50% of four-year-olds attending preschool from families earning less than $20,000 (NCES 1996). In addition, due primarily to inadequate funding, the quality of preschool and child care programs varies considerably, with studies finding that the majority of programs provide only mediocre quality and that only about 15% rate as good quality (Layzer, Goodson, & Moss 1993; Galinsky et al. 1994; Cost, Quality, & Child Outcomes Study Team 1995).

CONCLUSION

Collaboration between IRA and NAEYC is symbolic of the coming together of the two essential bodies of knowledge necessary to support literacy development of young children: knowledge about the processes of reading and writing and knowledge of child development and learning. Developmentally appropriate practices (Bredekamp & Copple 1997) in reading and writing are ways of teaching that consider

> **For children not progressing at grade level, schools need to focus on accelerating learning—through more intensive instructional strategies—rather than using grade retention or social promotion.**

1. what is generally known about children's development and learning to set achievable but challenging goals for literacy learning and to plan learning experiences and teaching strategies that vary with the age and experience of the learners;

2. results of ongoing assessment of individual children's progress in reading and writing to plan next steps or to adapt instruction when children fail to make expected progress or are at advanced levels; and

3. social and cultural contexts in which children live so as to help them make sense of their learning experiences in relation to what they already know and are able to do.

> **When children do not make expected progress in literacy, resources should be available to provide more individualized instruction, focused time, tutoring by qualified tutors, or other individualized intervention strategies.**

To teach in developmentally appropriate ways, teachers must understand *both* the continuum of reading and writing development *and* children's individual and cultural variations. Teachers must recognize when variation is within the typical range and when intervention is necessary, because early intervention is more effective and less costly than later remediation.

Learning to read and write is one of the most important and powerful achievements in life. Its value is clearly seen in the faces of young children—the proud, confident smile of the capable reader contrasts sharply with the furrowed brow and sullen frown of the discouraged nonreader. Ensuring that all young children reach their potentials as readers and writers is the shared responsibility of teachers, administrators, families, and communities. Educators have a special responsibility to teach every child and not to blame children, families, or each other when the task is difficult. All responsible adults need to work together to help children become competent readers and writers.

PHASE ONE

Awareness and Exploration (goals for preschool)

Children explore their environment and build the foundations for learning to read and write.

Children can

- enjoy listening to and discussing storybooks
- understand that print carries a message
- engage in reading and writing attempts
- identify labels and signs in their environment
- participate in rhyming games
- identify some letters and make some letter-sound matches
- use known letters or approximations of letters to represent written language (especially meaningful words like their name and phrases such as "I love you")

What teachers do

- share books with children, including Big Books, and model reading behaviors
- talk about letters by name and sounds
- establish a literacy-rich environment
- reread favorite stories
- engage children in language games
- promote literacy-related play activities
- encourage children to experiment with writing

What parents and family members can do

- talk with children, engage them in conversation, give names of things, show interest in what a child says
- read and reread stories with predictable texts to children
- encourage children to recount experiences and describe ideas and events that are important to them
- visit the library regularly
- provide opportunities for children to draw and print, using markers, crayons, and pencils

> This list is intended to be illustrative, not exhaustive. Children at any grade level will function at a variety of phases along the reading/writing continuum.

PHASE TWO

Experimental Reading and Writing (goals for kindergarten)

Children develop basic concepts of print and begin to engage in and experiment with reading and writing.

Kindergartners can

- enjoy being read to and themselves retell simple narrative stories or informational texts
- use descriptive language to explain and explore
- recognize letters and letter-sound matches
- show familiarity with rhyming and beginning sounds
- understand left-to-right and top-to-bottom orientation and familiar concepts of print
- match spoken words with written ones
- begin to write letters of the alphabet and some high-frequency words

What teachers do

- encourage children to talk about reading and writing experiences
- provide many opportunities for children to explore and identify sound-symbol relationships in meaningful contexts
- help children to segment spoken words into individual sounds and blend the sounds into whole words (for example, by slowly writing a word and saying its sound)
- frequently read interesting and conceptually rich stories to children

• provide daily opportunities for children to write
• help children build a sight vocabulary
• create a literacy-rich environment for children to engage independently in reading and writing

What parents and family members can do

• daily read and reread narrative and informational stories to children
• encourage children's attempts at reading and writing
• allow children to participate in activities that involve writing and reading (for example, cooking, making grocery lists)
• play games that involve specific directions (such as "Simon Says")
• have conversations with children during mealtimes and throughout the day

PHASE THREE

Early Reading and Writing (goals for first grade)

Children begin to read simple stories and can write about a topic that is meaningful to them.

First-graders can

• read and retell familiar stories
• use strategies (rereading, predicting, questioning, contextualizing) when comprehension breaks down
• use reading and writing for various purposes on their own initiative
• orally read with reasonable fluency
• use letter-sound associations, word parts, and context to identify new words
• identify an increasing number of words by sight
• sound out and represent all substantial sounds in spelling a word
• write about topics that are personally meaningful
• attempt to use some punctuation and capitalization

What teachers do

• support the development of vocabulary by reading daily to the children, transcribing their language, and selecting materials that expand children's knowledge and language development
• model strategies and provide practice for identifying unknown words
• give children opportunities for independent reading and writing practice
• read, write, and discuss a range of different text types (poems, informational books)
• introduce new words and teach strategies for learning to spell new words
• demonstrate and model strategies to use when comprehension breaks down
• help children build lists of commonly used words from their writing and reading

What parents and family members can do

• talk about favorite storybooks
• read to children and encourage them to read to you
• suggest that children write to friends and relatives
• bring to a parent-teacher's conference evidence of what your child can do in writing and reading
• encourage children to share what they have learned about their writing and reading

PHASE FOUR

Transitional Reading and Writing
(goals for second grade)

Children begin to read more fluently and write various text forms using simple and more complex sentences.

Second-graders can

• read with greater fluency

• use strategies more efficiently (rereading, questioning, and so on) when comprehension breaks down

• use word identification strategies with greater facility to unlock unknown words

• identify an increasing number of words by sight

• write about a range of topics to suit different audiences

• use common letter patterns and critical features to spell words

• punctuate simple sentences correctly and proofread their own work

• spend time reading daily and use reading to research topics

What teachers do

• create a climate that fosters analytic, evaluative, and reflective thinking

• teach children to write in multiple forms (stories, information, poems)

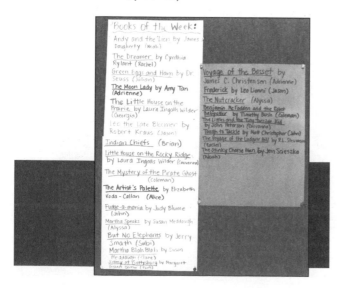

• ensure that children read a range of texts for a variety of purposes

• teach revising, editing, and proofreading skills

• teach strategies for spelling new and difficult words

• model enjoyment of reading

What parents and family members can do

• continue to read to children and encourage them to read to you

• engage children in activities that require reading and writing

• become involved in school activities

• show children your interest in their learning by displaying their written work

• visit the library regularly

• support your child's specific hobby or interest with reading materials and references

Early Reading and Writing

Children continue to extend and refine their reading and writing to suit varying purposes and audiences.

Third-graders can

• read fluently and enjoy reading

• use a range of strategies when drawing meaning from the text

• use word identification strategies appropriately and automatically when encountering unknown words

• recognize and discuss elements of different text structures

• make critical connections between texts

• write expressively in many different forms (stories, poems, reports)

• use a rich variety of vocabulary and sentences appropriate to text forms

• revise and edit their own writing during and after composing

• spell words correctly in final writing drafts

What teachers do

• provide opportunities daily for children to read, examine, and critically evaluate narrative and expository texts

• continue to create a climate that fosters critical reading and personal response

• teach children to examine ideas in texts

• encourage children to use writing as a tool for thinking and learning

• extend children's knowledge of the correct use of writing conventions

• emphasize the importance of correct spelling in finished written products

• create a climate that engages all children as a community of literacy learners

What parents and family members can do

• continue to support children's learning and interest by visiting the library and bookstores with them

• find ways to highlight children's progress in reading and writing

• stay in regular contact with your child's teachers about activities and progress in reading and writing

• encourage children to use and enjoy print for many purposes (such as recipes, directions, games, and sports)

• build a love of language in all its forms and engage children in conversation

References

Adams, M. 1990. *Beginning to read*. Cambridge, MA: MIT Press.

Anbar, A. 1986. Reading acquisition of preschool children without systematic instruction. *Early Childhood Research Quarterly* 1: 69–83.

Anderson, R.C. 1995. *Research foundations for wide reading*. Paper presented at invitational conference, "The Impact of Wide Reading," Center for the Study of Reading, Urbana, Illinois.

Applebee, A.N. 1977. Writing and reading. *Language Arts* 20: 534–37.

Barnett, W.S. 1995. Long-term effects of early childhood programs on cognitive and school outcomes. *The Future of Children* 5: 25–50.

Barron, R.W. 1980. Visual and phonological strategies in reading and spelling. In *Cognitive processes in spelling*, ed. U. Frith, 339–53. New York: Academic.

Berk, L. 1996. *Infants and children: Prenatal through middle childhood*. 2d ed. Boston: Allyn & Bacon.

Bissex, G. 1980. *GYNS AT WRK: A child learns to write and read*. Cambridge, MA: Harvard University Press.

Bond, G., & R. Dykstra. 1967. The cooperative research program in first-grade reading instruction. *Reading Research Quarterly* 2: 5–142.

Bradley, L., & P.E. Bryant. 1983. Categorizing sounds and learning to read: A causal connection. *Nature* 301: 419–21.

Bredekamp, S., & C. Copple, eds. 1997. *Developmentally appropriate practice in early childhood programs*. Rev. ed. Washington, DC: NAEYC.

Brown, A.L., & J.S. DeLoache. 1978. Skills, plans and self-regulation. In *Children's thinking: What develops?* ed. R. Siegler, 3–36. Hillsdale, NJ: Erlbaum.

Bryant, P.E., M. MacLean, L. Bradley, & J. Crossland. 1990. Rhyme and alliteration, phoneme detection, and learning to read. *Developmental Psychology* 26: 429–38.

Bryne, B., & R. Fielding-Barnsley. 1991. Evaluation of a program to teach phonemic awareness to young children. *Journal of Educational Psychology* 83: 451–55.

Bryne, B., & R. Fielding-Barnsley. 1993. Evaluation of a program to teach phonemic awareness to young children: A 1-year follow-up. *Journal of Educational Psychology* 85: 104–11.

Bryne, B., & R. Fielding-Barnsley. 1995. Evaluation of a program to teach phonemic awareness to young children: A 2- and 3-year follow-up and a new preschool trial. *Journal of Educational Psychology* 87: 488–503.

Bus, A., J. Belsky, M.H. van IJzendoorn, & K. Crnic. 1997. Attachment and book-reading patterns: A study of mothers, fathers, and their toddlers. *Early Childhood Research Quarterly* 12: 81–98.

Bus, A., & M. van IJzendoorn. 1995. Mothers reading to their 3-year-olds: The role of mother-child attachment security in becoming literate. *Reading Research Quarterly* 30: 998–1015.

Bus, A., M. van IJzendoorn, & A. Pellegrini. 1995. Joint book reading makes for success in learning to read: A meta-analysis on intergenerational transmission of literacy. *Review of Educational Research* 65: 1–21.

Chomsky, C. 1979. Approaching reading through invented spelling. In *Theory and practice of early reading*, vol. 2, eds. L.B. Resnick & P.A. Weaver, 43–65. Hillsdale, NJ: Erlbaum.

Clarke, L. 1988. Invented versus traditional spelling in first graders' writings: Effects on learning to spell and read. *Research in the Teaching of English* 22: 281–309.

Clay, M. 1975. *What did I write?* Portsmouth, NH: Heinemann.

Clay, M. 1979. *The early detection of reading difficulties*. Portsmouth, NH: Heinemann.

Clay, M. 1991. *Becoming literate*. Portsmouth, NH: Heinemann.

Cost, Quality, and Child Outcomes Study Team. 1995. *Cost, quality, and child outcomes in child care centers, public report*. 2d ed. Denver: Economics Department, University of Colorado.

Cummins, J. 1979. Linguistic interdependence and the educational development of bilingual children. *Review of Educational Research* 49: 222–51.

Cunningham, A. 1990. Explicit versus implicit instruction in phonemic awareness. *Journal of Experimental Child Psychology* 50: 429–44.

Darling-Hammond, L. 1997. *Doing what matters most: Investing in quality teaching*. New York: National Commission on Teaching and America's Future.

DEC/CEC (Division for Early Childhood of the Council for Exceptional Children). 1994. Position on inclusion. *Young Children* 49 (5): 78.

DEC (Division for Early Childhood) Task Force on Recommended Practices. 1993. *DEC recommended practices: Indicators of quality in programs for infants and young children with special needs and their families*. Reston, VA: Council for Exceptional Children.

Dickinson, D., & M. Smith. 1994. Long-term effects of preschool teachers' book readings on low-income children's vocabulary and story comprehension. *Reading Research Quarterly* 29: 104–22.

Domico, M.A. 1993. Patterns of development in narrative stories of emergent writers. In *Examining central issues in literacy research, theory, and practice*, eds. C. Kinzer & D. Leu, 391–404. Chicago: National Reading Conference.

Durkin, D. 1966. *Children who read early*. New York: Teachers College Press.

Durrell, D.D., & J.H. Catterson. 1980. *Durrell analysis of reading difficulty*. Rev. ed. New York: Psychological Corp.

Dyson, A.H. 1988. Appreciate the drawing and dictating of young children. *Young Children* 43 (3): 25–32.

Education Department of Western Australia. 1994. *Reading, writing, spelling, verbal language developmental continuum*. Portsmouth, NH: Heinemann.

Ehri, L. 1994. Development of the ability to read words: Update. In *Theoretical models and processes of reading*, eds. R. Ruddell, M.R. Ruddell, & H. Singer, 323–58. Newark, DE: International Reading Association.

Ehri, L.C., & C. Robbins. 1992. Beginners need some decoding skill to read words by analogy. *Reading Research Quarterly* 27: 13–26.

Ehri, L., & J. Sweet. 1991. Finger-point reading of memorized text: What enables beginners to process the print? *Reading Research Quarterly* 26: 442–61.

Elkonin, D.B. 1973. USSR. In *Comparative Reading,* ed. J. Downing, 551–80. New York: Macmillian.

Eller, R., C. Pappas, & E. Brown. 1988. The lexical development of kindergartners: Learning from written context. *Journal of Reading Behavior* 20: 5–24.

Elley, W. 1989. Vocabulary acquisition from listening to stories. *Reading Research Quarterly* 24: 174–87.

Feitelson, D., B. Kita, & Z. Goldstein. 1986. Effects of listening to series stories on first graders' comprehension and use of language. *Research in the Teaching of English* 20: 339–55.

Foorman, B., D. Novy, D. Francis, & D. Liberman. 1991. How letter-sound instruction mediates progress in first-grade reading and spelling. *Journal of Educational Psychology* 83: 456–69.

Galinsky, E., C. Howes, S. Kontos., & M. Shinn. 1994. *The study of children in family child care and relative care: Highlights of findings.* New York: Families and Work Institute.

Gibson, E., & E. Levin. 1975. *The psychology of reading.* Cambridge, MA: MIT Press.

Graves, D. 1983. *Writing: Teachers and children at work.* Portsmouth, NH: Heinemann.

Hannon, P. 1995. *Literacy, home and school.* London: Falmer.

Hanson, R., & D. Farrell. 1995. The long-term effects on high school seniors of learning to read in kindergarten. *Reading Research Quarterly* 30: 908–33.

Hart, B., & T. Risley. 1995. *Meaningful differences.* Baltimore: Brookes.

Henderson, E.H., & J.W. Beers. 1980. *Developmental and cognitive aspects of learning to spell.* Newark, DE: International Reading Association,

Holdaway, D. 1979. *The foundations of literacy .* Portsmouth, NH: Heinemann.

Howes, C., D.A. Phillips, & M. Whitebook. 1992. Thresholds of quality: Implications for the social development of children in center-based child care. *Child Development* 63: 449–60.

IRA (International Reading Association). 1998. *Phonics in the early reading program: A position statement.* Newark, DE: Author.

Johnston, P. 1997. *Knowing literacy: Constructive literacy assessment.* York, ME: Stenhouse.

Juel, C. 1991. Beginning reading. In *Handbook of reading research,* vol. 2, eds. R. Barr, M. Kamil, P. Mosenthal, & P.D. Pearson, 759–88. New York: Longman.

Juel, C., P.L. Griffith, & P. Gough. 1986. Acquisition of literacy: A longitudinal study of children in first and second grade. *Journal of Educational Psychology* 78: 243–55.

Kagan, S.L., & N. Cohen. 1997. *Not by chance: Creating an early care and education system for America's children.* New Haven, CT: Bush Center in Child Development and Social Policy, Yale University.

Karweit, N., & B. Wasik. 1996. The effects of story reading programs on literacy and language development of disadvantaged pre-schoolers. *Journal of Education for Students Placed At-Risk* 4: 319–48.

Katz, L., & C. Chard. 1989. *Engaging children's minds.* Norwood, NJ: Ablex.

Layzer, J., B. Goodson, & M. Moss. 1993. *Life in preschool: Volume one of an observational study of early childhood programs for disadvantaged four-year-olds.* Cambridge, MA: Abt Associates.

Leung, C.B., & J.J. Pikulski. 1990. Incidental learning of word meanings by kindergarten and first grade children thorough repeated read aloud events. In *Literacy theory and research: Analyses from multiple paradigms,* eds. J. Zutell & S. McCormick, 231–40. Chicago: National Reading Conference.

Lundberg, I., J. Frost, & O.P. Petersen. 1988. Effects of an extensive program for stimulating phonological awareness in preschool children. *Reading Research Quarterly* 23: 263–84.

Maclean, M., P. Bryant, & L. Bradley. 1987. Rhymes, nursery rhymes, and reading in early childhood. *Merrill-Palmer Quarterly* 33: 255–81.

Mason, J. 1980. When do children begin to read: An exploration of four-year-old children's word reading competencies. *Reading Research Quarterly* 15: 203–27.

Mason, J., & S. Sinha. 1993. Emerging literacy in the early childhood years: Applying a Vygotskian model of learning and development. In *Handbook of research on the education of young children,* ed. B. Spodek, 137–50. New York: Macmillian.

McGee, L., R. Lomax, & M. Head. 1988. Young children's written language knowledge: What environmental and functional print reading reveals. *Journal of Reading Behavior* 20: 99–118.

McGee, L., & D. Richgels. 1996. *Literacy's beginnings.* Boston: Allyn & Bacon.

McGill-Franzen, A., & C. Lanford. 1994. Exposing the edge of the preschool curriculum: Teachers' talk about text and children's literary understandings. *Language Arts* 71: 264–73.

Morrow, L.M. 1988. Young children's responses to one-to-one readings in school settings. *Reading Research Quarterly* 23: 89–107.

Morrow, L.M. 1990. Preparing the classroom environment to promote literacy during play. *Early Childhood Research Quarterly* 5: 537–54.

Morrow, L.M., D. Strickland, & D.G. Woo. 1998. *Literacy instruction in half- and whole-day kindergarten.* Newark, DE: International Reading Association.

Morrow, L.M., & C. Weinstein. 1986. Encouraging voluntary reading: The impact of a literature program on children's use of library centers. *Reading Research Quarterly* 21: 330–46.

Moyer, S.B. 1982. Repeated reading. *Journal of Learning Disabilities* 15: 619–23.

NAEYC. 1996a. NAEYC position statement: Responding to linguistic and cultural diversity—Recommendations for effective early childhood education. *Young Children* 51 (2): 4–12.

NAEYC. 1996b. NAEYC position statement: Technology and young children—Ages three through eight. *Young Children* 51 (6): 11–16.

NCES (National Center for Education Statistics). 1996. *The condition of education.* Washington, DC: U.S. Department of Education.

Neuman, S.B. 1997. Literary research that makes a difference: A study of access to literacy. *Reading Research Quarterly* 32 (April–June): 202–10.

Neuman, S.B. 1998. How can we enable all children to achieve? In *Children achieving: Best practices in early literacy,* eds. S.B. Neuman & K. Roskos. Newark, DE: International Reading Association.

Neuman, S.B., & K. Roskos. 1992. Literacy objects as cultural tools: Effects on children's literacy behaviors in play. *Reading Research Quarterly* 27: 202–25.

Neuman, S.B., & K. Roskos. 1993. Access to print for children of poverty: Differential effects of adult mediation and literacy-enriched play settings on environmental and functional print tasks. *American Educational Research Journal* 30: 95–122.

Neuman, S.B., & K. Roskos. 1997. Literacy knowledge in practice: Contexts of participation for young writers and readers. *Reading Research Quarterly* 32: 10–32.

Nye, B.A., J. Boyd-Zaharias, & B.D. Fulton. 1994. *The lasting benefits study: A continuing analysis of the effect of small class size in kindergarten through third grade on student achievement test scores in subsequent grade levels—seventh grade (1992–93): Technical report.* Nashville: Center of Excellence for Research in Basic Skills, Tennessee State University.

Nye, B.A., J. Boyd-Zaharias, B.D. Fulton, & M.P. Wallenhorst. 1992. Smaller classes really are better. *The American School Board Journal* 179 (5): 31–33.

Pappas, C. 1991. Young children's strategies in learning the "book language" of information books. *Discourse Processes* 14: 203–25.

Read, C. 1971. Pre-school children's knowledge of English phonology. *Harvard Educational Review* 41: 1–34.

Richgels, D.J. 1986. Beginning first graders' "invented spelling" ability and their performance in functional classroom writing activities. *Early Childhood Research Quarterly* 1: 85–97.

Richgels, D.J. 1995. Invented spelling ability and printed word learning in kindergarten. *Reading Research Quarterly* 30: 96–109.

Riley, J. 1996. *The teaching of reading.* London: Paul Chapman.

Roberts, B. 1998. "I No EvrethENGe": What skills are essential in early literacy? In *Children achieving: Best practices in early literacy,* eds. S.B. Neuman & K. Roskos, 38–55. Newark, DE: International Reading Association.

Rowe, D.W. 1994. *Preschoolers as authors.* Cresskill, NJ: Hampton.

Samuels, S.J. 1979. The method of repeated readings. *The Reading Teacher* 32: 403–08.

Shepard, L. 1994. The challenges of assessing young children appropriately. *Phi Delta Kappan* 76: 206–13.

Shepard, L., S.L. Kagan, & E. Wurtz, eds. 1998. *Principles and recommendations for early childhood assessments.* Washington, DC: National Education Goals Panel.

Shepard, L., & M.L. Smith. 1988. Escalating academic demand in kindergarten: Some nonsolutions. *Elementary School Journal* 89: 135–46.

Shepard, L., & M.L. Smith. 1989. *Flunking grades: Research and policies on retention.* Bristol, PA: Taylor & Francis.

Snow, C. 1991. The theoretical basis for relationships between language and literacy in development. *Journal of Research in Childhood Education* 6: 5–10.

Snow, C., M.S. Burns, & P. Griffin. 1998. *Preventing reading difficulties in young children.* Washington, DC: National Academy Press.

Snow, C., P. Tabors, P. Nicholson, & B. Kurland. 1995. SHELL: Oral language and early literacy skills in kindergarten and first-grade children. *Journal of Research in Childhood Education* 10: 37–48.

Stanovich, K.E. 1986. Matthew Effects in reading: Some consequences of individual differences in the acquisition of literacy. *Reading Research Quarterly* 21: 360–406.

Stanovich, K.E., & R.F. West. 1989. Exposure to print and orthographic processing. *Reading Research Quarterly* 24: 402–33.

Stauffer, R. 1970. *The language experience approach to the teaching of reading.* New York: Harper & Row.

Strickland, D. 1994. Educating African American learners at risk: Finding a better way. *Language Arts* 71: 328–36.

Sulzby, E. 1985. Kindergartners as writers and readers. In *Advances in writing research,* ed. M.Farr, 127–99. Norwood, NJ: Ablex.

Teale, W. 1984. Reading to young children: Its significance for literacy development. In *Awakening to literacy,* eds. H. Goelman, A. Oberg, & F. Smith, 110–21. Portsmouth, NH: Heinemann.

Tierney, R., & T. Shanahan. 1991. Research on the reading-writing relationship: Interactions, transactions, and outcomes. In *Handbook on reading research,* vol. 2, eds. R. Barr, M. Kamil, P. Mosenthal, & P.D. Pearson, 246–80. New York: Longman.

Vernon-Feagans, L., D. Emanuel, & I. Blood. 1992. About middle ear problems: The effect of otitis media and quality of day care on children's language development. *Journal of Applied Developmental Psychology* 18: 395–409.

Vukelich, C. 1994. Effects of play interventions on young children's reading of environmental print. *Early Childhood Research Quarterly* 9: 153–70.

Wagner, R., & J. Torgesen. 1987. The nature of phonological processing and its causal role in the acquisition of reading skills. *Psychological Bulletin* 101: 192–212.

Wells, G. 1985. *The meaning makers.* Portsmouth, NH: Heinemann.

Whitehurst, G., D. Arnold, J. Epstein, A. Angell, M. Smith, & J. Fischel. 1994. A picture book reading intervention in day care and home for children from low-income families. *Developmental Psychology* 30: 679–89.

Whitmore, K., & Y. Goodman. 1995. Transforming curriculum in language and literacy. In *Reaching potentials: Transforming early childhood curriculum and assessment,* vol. 2, eds. S. Bredekamp & T. Rosegrant, 145–66. Washington, DC: NAEYC.

Wong Fillmore, L. 1991. When learning a second language means losing the first. *Early Childhood Research Quarterly* 6: 323–46.

Section 2:

READERS AND WRITERS IN THE MAKING

The Power and Pleasure of Literacy

The Literate Environment

Language Development

Building Knowledge and Comprehension

Knowledge of Print

Types of Text

Phonological Development

Letters and Words

Taking Stock

Beginning in infancy and continuing throughout childhood, children may learn from those around them that in language and literacy there is much value, enjoyment, and sheer power. If they do not develop such an interest in reading and writing—an eager desire for initiation into print's mysteries and skills—children's progress toward literacy is uncertain. When the going gets tough, they may drop out of the game.

While eagerness does not guarantee success, motivated children are far more likely to persist and succeed than are children who see no point in all the hard work of learning to read and write.

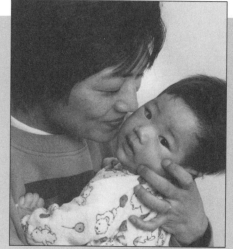

The path to literacy begins with very simple adult behaviors that infants and toddlers find interesting or pleasing. Caregivers may respond to babies' cooing, babbling, and other vocalizations; speak in warm, expressive voices in attending to children's needs and playing with them; and recite nursery rhymes and other chants or verses with appealing rhythms and sound patterns.

Baby: *Ba-ba-ba-ba-ba.*

Caregiver (stroking the infant's tummy and smiling): *Is that right? Ba-ba-ba-ba-ba. You're a happy baby today—yes, you are!*

Children of all ages love the intimacy of reading with an adult, either one-on-one or with only a few other children. Teachers and caregivers should seek out daily opportunities to read with every child. And since regular reading at home is a potent force in promoting children's literacy, any actions teachers take to encourage parents' reading with children can reap substantial long-term benefits.

Group storytime should be a warm, relaxed interlude. Preschoolers like to participate in selecting the book, adding sound effects and actions, and chiming in when they know the next word or phrase. With older children the teacher's reading aloud from a spellbinding chapter book often entices them to tackle more challenging material.

Children are more likely to become good readers and writers when they repeatedly encounter—both in and out of the classroom—the many ways that reading and writing matter. Seeing teachers and other adults read for their own enjoyment and information and write and use print in their work and leisure—these experiences convey to children a powerful message about literacy's pleasures and rewards.

Using items such as notepads and pencils, memos, and magazines in their dramatic play makes young children feel like readers and writers. Whether they are pretending or practicing these skills—or perhaps doing a bit of both—children use such play to progress toward fully developed literacy.

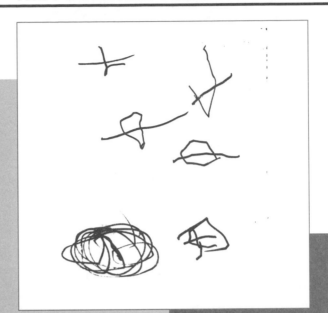

As children begin to recognize that by writing they can make real things happen, their interest soars. In dozens of ways they flex their muscles as producers of print. For instance, in the messages shown here, children are laying hold of an exciting and useful power: communication with people one won't be seeing face-to-face.

Sasha (3½ years) prepares a note for the oven repairman; Matt (5) leaves crystal-clear instructions for Santa; and Jake (6) posts a sign on the trash can in case his missing toy ax was thrown out by mistake.

Children are eager to do what grown-ups do. Just seeing how reading and writing twine through adults' work and leisure activities is in itself compelling. But when a child takes on the part of a grown-up in play, she steps into the active role of reader and writer. For the child's future in reading and writing, this is strong stuff.

Teachers can ensure that children have many such experiences right in the classroom. The dramatic-play themes, props, and materials suggested here are only a fraction of what's possible.

Post Office

Envelopes of various sizes
Stationery, postcards
Pens, pencils, markers
Stickers, stamps, stamp pads
Post office mailbox
Tote bag to carry mail
Computer address labels
Tape
Calendars
Small drawer trays
Posters and signs about mailing
Mail carrier's cap
Newspaper ads from drugstores, department stores, furniture stores
Mailboxes for each child and adult
Stapler

Office

Appointment book
Message pads
Stapler
File folders
Racks for filing papers
In/out trays
Index cards
Business cards
Assorted forms
Desk and wall calendars
Computer and printer
Clipboards
Note cards, sticky notes, address labels
Paper clips of various sizes
Pens, pencils, markers
Organizing trays for holding items
Brochures, pamphlets

Construction Company (Block Play)

Order forms
Pencils
Hard hats
Toolboxes
Canvas aprons for carrying tools
Mobile phones
Catalogs and advertisements from hardware and home supply stores
Photos, postcards, drawings, blueprints, and pictures of buildings under construction and completed
Books showing construction stages of buildings
Markers and cardboard for making signs
Additional blocks—flat boards, arches, wedges, cylinders, etc.
Trucks and machinery—delivery truck, dump truck, backhoe, crane, bulldozer
Books showing uses of various tools and vehicles

Pizza Restaurant

Cash register
Play money
Small pizza boxes
Round pizza pan
Pizza cutter
Wooden paddle
Twelve-inch cardboard circle to serve as a pizza pattern
Red, yellow, green, brown, and tan construction paper for making pizzas
Order pads, receipt book
Pencils, pens
Menus listing 5 to 10 items with prices
Telephone
Soda cups
Small chalkboard and chalk to list specials
Apron or shirt and cap
Red checkered tablecloth

Library

Library book return cards
Stamps for dating return cards
Wide variety of children's books
Bookmarks
Pens, pencils, markers
Paper of assorted sizes
Sign-in/sign-out sheet
Stickers
ABC index cards for card file drawers
Telephone
Telephone books
Calendars of various types
Posters of children's books
File folders

Bookstore

Cash register
Stick-on price tags
Pens, pencils, markers
Posters, book jackets from children's books
Shelf or table for arranging books by author or genre (stories, real things, poetry, music, etc.)
Order pad
Computer keyboard
Tape recorder, earphones, and books on tape
Bags to hold purchases

Supermarket

Cash register with tape
Play money
Grocery advertisement fliers
Plastic food items or cutouts mounted on boards and covered with clear contact paper or plastic wrap
Empty food containers—cereal boxes, egg cartons, milk containers, plastic juice bottles, Styrofoam meat trays, and so on
Stick-on price tags
Plastic and paper bags
Child-size shopping cart and basket
Signs collected from stores
Crayons and markers for making signs
Paper, scissors, tape
Aprons, jackets

Adapted from The University of the State of New York/ The State Education Department. 1998. *Preschool planning guide: Building a foundation for development of language and literacy in the early years*, 22–23. Albany, NY: Author. Used with permission.

Story Day

In her preschool class Elizabeth Kirk developed a weekly Story Day, when a small number of children dictate stories to the teacher and later have them performed for the class. In advance she posts a list of the day's storytellers, ensuring that each child has an opportunity to create a story. Going to one child at a time, Ms. Kirk asks, "Would you like to tell a story today?" and then writes down the storyteller's dictation.

Watching the teacher write his very own words, the child is able to observe formation of letter shapes, left-to-right progression, and spacing between words. Even very young children begin to understand that print relates to spoken words. And as the teacher reads back the child's words, he begins to grasp that what is written can also be read.

To make Story Day as enjoyable and productive as possible for children, Ms. Kirk finds these guidelines for teachers useful:

• Offer comments and questions only when needed—for instance, "Stories sometimes start with 'Once upon time'" or "What did the kitten and princess do together?"

• Be sure to allow the story to come from the child, without altering her words or imposing your ideas. If a child gets stuck, read back the last portion so he remembers what has happened and can go on with the next segment.

• Because it is best to limit stories to a single page, alert the storyteller as her dictation approaches the bottom of the page to allow her time to wrap up the story. This also focuses attention on story endings and, over time, on structuring a story rather than just meandering along.

• When a child is ready to learn more about print, highlight a name or key word in his completed story, pointing it out wherever it appears in the narrative.

At storytime, the teacher asks each of the day's authors, "Would you like to act out your story today?" (Some may want only to hear the story read aloud.) The author then can choose a role for himself and select characters from among his peers to dramatize the story ("Lupita, will you be the cat?").

When reading the story aloud to the class, the teacher should read slowly and pause long enough to allow the characters to interpret the actions however they choose.

Children are an appreciative audience, delighting in each production, and their applause encourages others' participation. Soon each child eagerly anticipates his or her next opportunity to tell a story.

Story Day stimulates and hones children's narrative skills and their awareness of print's connections to language. For children learning English the dictation and dramatization process is especially helpful.

Elizabeth W. Kirk, a preschool teacher and administrator, has encouraged children to dictate and dramatize their own stories for more than 15 years. For more detailed information on how she uses Story Day in her own classroom, see Kirk, E.W. 1998. My favorite day is Story Day. *Young Children* 53 (6): 27–30.

Nomad's Visit

Throughout the school year a well-worn toy dog named Nomad goes home with a different child each weekend, taking along the journal in which the child writes their shared adventures on the visit. If the child is not writing yet, the instructions inside the journal's cover ask parents to record their child's account of what Nomad does while visiting. Before beginning her entry or afterward, the child often wants to read, or have read to her, some of Nomad's doings at other children's houses.

During circle time the next day, the child (or teacher if necessary) reads Nomad's entry to the group. Other children like to ask questions and chime in enthusiastically with what Nomad did at their homes.

This idea was used by Stephanie Rubin with her third- and fourth-grade class at the Friends Community School in College Park, Maryland. The same concept, designed for preschoolers, is described in *Young Children*. See Rowley, R. 1999. Caregivers' Corner. A visiting puppet. *Young Children* 54 (4): 21.

Book Hospital

Well-used books are well-loved books. But sometimes for all their good intentions, young children can smudge, tear, and bend them. A book hospital "where books go to get better" teaches children to value books and take good care of them.

In a corner of the library area or the publishing center, use an old crate, or sturdy box as a container to collect books that are in need of repair. Useful items to include in the hospital: invisible tape for ripped pages or flaps, art gum erasers to remove crayon and pencil marks from glossy pages, and glue to repair paper torn off cardboard book covers or board book pages. Also have heavy-duty book tape on hand to repair broken spines—glue the tape down the outside of the spine, on the inside front and back seams, and on the center seam.

Don't forget disinfectant to clean dirty books. Fill spray bottles with 10 parts water to one part ammonia or alcohol. Dab the diluted solution on a paper towel to wipe off covers and board books. For use of possibly toxic materials like disinfectant and rubber cement, it is advisable to wait until children have gone for the day.

When first introducing the book hospital, invite a few children at a time to watch you do repairs. Then they can take turns helping or make simple repairs as you look on or assist in determining what each book needs.

Through the book hospital children learn to take responsibility for fixing and restoring the things they use and want to enjoy.

Young children's learning environments should be rich in print. But more doesn't always mean better. In a room cluttered with labels, signs, and such—print for print's sake—letters and words become just so much wallpaper. Likewise, having lots and lots of books is wonderful, but not if they are out of children's reach.

Put labels, captions, and other print in the places that count: where they catch children's attention and where they serve a purpose. For instance, "We'll need signs to help us tell the long and short ropes apart" or "There's room in the loft for only three kids at a time, so don't go up if three name cards are already on the board."

Teachers and administrators should ensure that, whatever children's cultural experiences have been, all children and their families will find much to make them feel at home in the early childhood program.

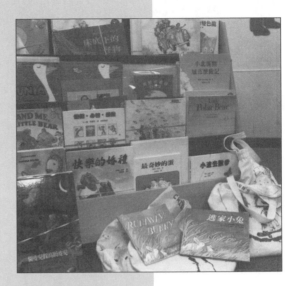

Equally important, children should encounter much to increase their comfort and competence within the classroom culture and their acquaintance with other cultures.

Make sure your classroom contains a variety of books, pictures, and print that affirm children's family experiences and their cultural and linguistic backgrounds. In such an environment children's engagement and progress in literacy increase. Conversely, if materials and tasks devalue or ignore children's cultural and linguistic identities, the gap widens between the classroom and the home and neighborhood.

Where do butterflies go when it rains?

¿A donde van las mariposas cuando llueve?

"Van para su casa donde viven las bumble bees." Uriel

"Home to a big tree in Victory Park." Eloisa.

"I don't know, maybe to my house or inside my plant." Dominique

"Se van a las nubes con Diosito." Saul

"Al cielo con su mama grande y se tapan con las nubes." Damian

"They go to a tree house that God made for them and for the kids too." Courtlin

"Van para afuera y cierran la puerta." Ignacio

"They go to Villa Parke and sleep." Shannon

"A los árboles, abren las puertas con las Chipendales." Ricardo

"A los aviones por un hueco se metan y se quedan allí." Jorge C.

"En el piso de la casa." Rosario

"Se van con las flores y se metan abajo." Sarai

For mobile infants and toddlers, books are kept on low shelves and in baskets. Books need to be sturdy and washable, since very young children are likely to tear and pull at pages and put books in their mouths. Stiff cardboard pages are easier for babies and toddlers to turn than are pages of cloth or vinyl.

Children love comfortable, cozy places where they can sit and read by themselves or with a friend or perhaps a favorite bear. Displaying books on open shelves with the covers visible invites children's interest.

A literate classroom offers abundant opportunities for children to make use of print and practice literacy habits and skills throughout the environment. For instance, when dramatic-play areas contain literacy-related props, children write (or pretend to write) lists, notes, signs, prescriptions, price tags, menus, and more. When teachers rotate materials to stimulate and support varying play themes, children get fresh opportunities to broaden their vocabulary and social knowledge.

As children cook, they consult recipes and examine the marks on measuring spoons. In the block area they use writing materials to make signs and the like. Wherever children do science, notepads, drawing paper, and writing tools are on hand for recording observations, sketching, and labeling specimens. And so, throughout the room and across the curriculum, teachers find ways to add print, props, and writing materials to enhance the language and literacy learning that occurs in play.

You've Got Mail!

"I got a letter!" James says as he reaches into the class mailbox.

Casey points to the message board and says, "Hey, look! This says we're going on a boat ride on Friday!"

Jessica drops a note into the suggestion box: "Get more blocks. We run out of the big ones."

These children are having authentic first-hand experiences participating in the world of print. To set the scene for such experiences, try these ideas and add variations of your own. (*Two tips:* Be sure to keep plenty of writing materials available in each area, and make frequent additions and changes to keep things from getting stale).

• Create a **message board** for reminders, morning messages, bulletins, and exchange of personal notes and ideas.

• Using cardboard boxes, construct one or more small-scale **kiosks** on which to post invitations, announcements, sketches, and reminders.

• Set up a **suggestion box** for children to share ideas, recommendations, and complaints.

• Make individual **mailboxes** or pigeonholes for each child and adult—using shoe boxes, cereal boxes, or stackable crates. Send notes to the children and encourage them to write messages to classmates, teachers, and parents. Whether children put messages directly into others' boxes or you designate daily mail carriers to make the deliveries, children get lots of practice recognizing classmates' and teachers' names.

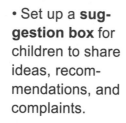

Teachers' interactions with children engaged in using these methods of communicating will naturally vary depending upon the children's progress in acquiring reading and writing skills. Whatever their writing capabilities, children crafting messages often ask adults and peers, "How do you write_____?" And children want teachers' help—more at first, less later—in interpreting the messages they receive.

When a classroom offers regular ways to send and receive messages, teachers and children interact often about print. Better still, these interactions occur at "motivated moments"—when the child is eager to make out what a message says or when she is struggling to communicate something to another person. The teacher can see what is difficult for the child at this point in time and what is just within reach, and she can provide the scaffolding—questions, hints, and help—that enables her to move forward.

Sometimes the teacher may simply take dictation from a child wishing to send a note or may read a message to the child who received it and needs help interpreting it. She may point to key words or offer comments ("See, there's *your* name, and there's where he wrote *his* name"). On other occasions the teacher may involve children in examining the print. For instance, with a child just beginning to recognize letters, she may say, "Do you see any letters or words you know?" or "What word do you think this could be?"

Literacy Outdoors

Paulo is standing in the middle of the trike path with his hand up. "Stop!" he tells Rosa as she rides up. "You are going too fast. You need a ticket." He writes on his palm with an imaginary pencil and hands her an imaginary ticket. "That's $500." Rosa takes the ticket, reaches into her pocket, and places some imaginary money in Paulo's hand.

Children sometimes include in their play various acts of reading or writing. They may make use of an item that comes to hand—using a small stick for a pencil, for example—or they may pretend, using actions only, as Paulo and Rosa did.

Such literate moments during outdoor play increase when the environment includes real tools for reading and writing, as well as literacy-related props. Maps can be taped to the fence for all to consult, or they can be placed in pouches with shoulder straps so children can easily carry them along on their travels. Signs can be added to the playyard as well: traffic signs along the pathway, labeling signs to turn part of the yard into a fast food restaurant, a post office, or a fire station. Bringing paper, markers, and tape outside allows children to create their own signs.

The larger scale of the great outdoors affects the types of props to be brought out. For example, the small envelopes used for a classroom post office would be easily lost in the yard. Playyard postal workers can deliver instead big packages, corrugated postcards made from sides of boxes, and letters in large, page-size brown envelopes.

From *Emergent Literacy and Dramatic Play in Early Education, 1st edition,* by J.I. Davidson. © 1996. Reprinted with permission of Delmar Publishers, a division of Thomson Learning. Fax 800 730-2215.

Keep Things Fresh...

Adding literacy-related props and tools to various areas of the classroom is a great way to integrate literacy concepts and functions into dramatic play. But it is easy to fall into a rut, using the same provisions until they become stale and uninteresting to children. Create variety by supplying an assortment of materials to different play areas. Have small pads available in the restaurant area for taking customers' orders, large sheets of paper and tape in the grocery store area for making signs and price tags, clipboards in the doctor's area for noting patients' symptoms, and notebooks in the science area for recording findings. And take care to rotate materials on a regular basis to keep things fresh.

The Library Center

Children learn to love reading when they have many opportunities to look at books independently, with adults, and with friends in a library corner. They delight in revisiting favorite books, turning the pages and pretending to read, and reenacting the books with others. A cozy area in the classroom, with books easily accessible, entices children to read and read often.

In the classroom library, various features help to encourage children's use of books:

• Partition an area in the room using semi-fixed structures like bookshelves, cabinets, or freestanding bulletin boards. The space should accommodate four or five children.

• Add comfortable seating, rugs, big pillows, and stuffed animals to lend softness to the area.

• Use open-face bookracks so that children can see the covers of the books.

• Put out a variety of books, magazines, and other reading material at one time.

• Provide many types of reading material, including information books, stories, poetry, alphabet and counting books, and wordless picture books—and those wonderful volumes published by the children themselves.

• Display the children's work, posters, and other literacy materials. (For free posters, write the American Library Association, 50 East Huron Street, Chicago, IL 60611.)

• Add cassette players, headphones, and tapes for listening to stories.

• Include props such as library tickets and book pockets, in/out trays, pretend eyeglasses, and rubber stamps to encourage library-related play.

• With help from the children, create a special name for their library center.

Even when there is a school library, every classroom needs a library center of its own. Classroom libraries should include a wide variety of books that span a significant range of difficulty: books that fall within the easy-reading level of all the children, books that are challenging for everyone, and books at all points along the easy-to-challenging reading continuum.

The books to be found in a classroom at any given time include the permanent collection and a revolving collection that changes every few weeks, based on the topics being studied and the children's current interests. While you'll undoubtedly make regular use of the public library, you may also want to build up an assortment of books that can stay in the classroom year-round. Try visiting flea markets and tag sales, and encourage parents to donate books. And don't overlook the sales held regularly at local library branches.

In the classroom library should be traditional fables, folktales, and fantasies, as well as information and realistic fiction. Try to include reading material in the home languages spoken by the children and their families. It is important to provide an array of books that reflects the diverse, multicultural nature of our society, books in which children can see themselves and others.

Book clubs such as Troll, Grolier, and Scholastic offer excellent selections of children's books at lower cost than bookstores. When parents order through these clubs, children's home access to books is increased and the teacher gets bonus points to exchange for free classroom books (check out troll.com, scholastic.com, and grolier.com on the Internet). And find out whether you are eligible for the Reading Is Fundamental program (1-877-RIF-READ), which offers free book distribution for classroom libraries.

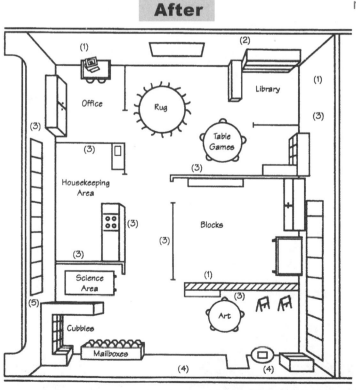

Before

Posters
Blackboard
Calendar
Computer
Small Toys
Posters
Rug
Manipulatives
Science Area
Housekeeping Area
Blocks
Sand/Water Table
Table Games
Art
Cubbies

The "Before" and "After" diagrams illustrate how teachers can transform a classroom environment into one that supports greater literacy learning. The various activity areas of the classroom (see "Before") are ill defined, with few closed spaces and partitions, and are not labeled. There is limited access to books, writing materials, and other literacy-related items.

Contrast this setting with the literacy-enriched environment ("After"). Now the teachers have more clearly defined the various areas by using cupboards, screens, tables, and written signs. They have labeled items throughout the environment and added a library center and other literacy-related features, such as mailboxes. In the dramatic play and block areas, props and writing materials are provided to spark children to incorporate reading and writing in their play.

After

(1)
(2)
(1)
Office
Library
Rug
(3)
(3)
(3)
Table Games
(3)
Housekeeping Area
(3)
(3)
Blocks
(3)
(3)
Science Area
(1)
(3)
(5)
Art
Cubbies
Mailboxes
(4)
(4)

Key		
Print		
(1) Children's writing + plans		
(2) Book jackets + posters by illustrators		
(3) Environmental and informational print		
(4) Children's artwork + art inventory		
(5) Science observations		
Other		
|——| — low divider		

Adapted from Neuman, S.B. & K. Roskos. 1993. *Language and literacy learning in the early years,* 109–10. Fort Worth, TX: Harcourt Brace Jovanich. Used with permission.

In learning to read and write, the role of children's language skills and word knowledge cannot be overestimated. Although children are "hard-wired" to acquire language, they require environments in which they experience language used in meaningful contexts. The variety of language that children experience, as well as the quantity, matters. And the ways people use language, at home and in early childhood settings, also shape what each child brings to literacy learning.

We foster young children's developing language when we talk, sing, and interact with them throughout the day, during routines as well as during play. Not only for language but also for social and cognitive development, nothing is more crucial than our responsiveness to what children do and say. And in these early back-and-forth exchanges, children learn the interactive game that is conversation.

Children need language to grow on. We supply words that describe their actions ("Look, Sarah is adding a red block").

When the child makes a remark, we respond by building on the remark but adding a bit more; that is, we use the child's words and topic but augment, fill in, elaborate.

Talia (2½): *Drink milk.* (hands the caregiver an empty plastic teacup)

Caregiver: *Thank you! Let me drink this good milk.*

All children benefit from experiences that expand their language skills and stock of words. For children with underdeveloped language and vocabulary, however, we must provide even more extensive language experience; there is ground to make up. At every opportunity we make a point of talking and reading with them and thus introduce a steady flow of new words, concepts, and linguistic structures.

But how do we increase the odds of children actually adding the new words they hear to their vocabulary? To convey and highlight meaning, it is often helpful to point to the pictured object, add a gesture, give a simple explanation.

Children's delight in jokes and riddles, silly verses, and all sorts of verbal play reflects their natural playfulness with language, which as teachers we want to actively nurture. Share with children the work of the great players-with-language like Dr. Seuss, Edmund Lear, and A.A. Milne. Engage them in silly songs and fingerplays and encourage them to add their own verses and variations. Grab a marker and record the language play and inventions so children can return to enjoy them—and perhaps build on them—at a later time.

Dramatic play is fertile ground for children's use of language. By introducing new themes and materials, and sometimes by taking a role in the play, we multiply the amazing potential of play to foster children's language capabilities and build vocabulary.

A bit of adult engagement and modeling of play behaviors is also key in helping less skilled children progress to the kind of rich sociodramatic play in which the most sustained, complex language interaction occurs.

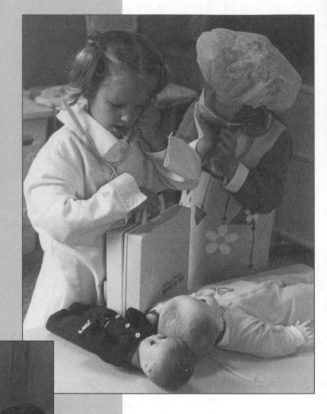

May I take your order?

Seeing two girls pretending to peruse menus, the teacher notices that no one has taken on the role of waiter. "May I take your order, ladies?" she asks, notepad in hand, and thus introduces a new script, a fresh possibility for play.

Over the next few days, the children add more to the waiter's role—bringing out plates of food, giving the cook orders, and writing out bills for the diners. The teacher's brief moment of involvement has enhanced the richness of the children's social and language interactions and sparked their use of writing for new purposes.

When doing individual seatwork, children are silent and solitary. Working collaboratively, by contrast, requires children to continually use and respond to language. Children explain, describe, challenge, negotiate. When others misunderstand, the child continues to search for words that communicate his meaning.

Books Without Words

In *Pancakes for Breakfast,* Tomie dePaola charmingly presents the story of an old woman as she makes pancakes—without using a single word. Children enjoy Mercer Mayer's *Frog, Where Are You?* which is about a little boy's adventure as he looks for his frog. Books like these tell a story through illustrations only.

One of the beauties of wordless books is that children themselves become the storytellers. Each time a child goes through such a book, she tells the story somewhat differently. She uses her developing vocabulary, creativity, and knowledge of narratives to elaborate, explore, and refine the story.

Books without words have other benefits. Because the pictures are arranged consecutively on each page, young children get a sense of left-to-right organization. They also get practice handling books and experience examining pictures as they read.

By writing down the stories that children compose as they "read" wordless books, then assisting these young authors in turning their stories into books, teachers nourish children's sense of themselves as readers and writers.

Many of the following authors, including Goodall, McCully, Mayer, Spier, and Tafuri, have numerous other recommendable titles.

Bang, M. 1980. *The grey lady and the strawberry snatcher.* New York: Four Winds.

Bonners, S. 1989. *Just in passing.* New York: Lothrop, Lee & Shepard.

Brown, C. 1989. *The patchwork farmer.* New York: Greenwillow.

Cristini, E., & L. Puricelli. 1984. *In the pond.* New York: Picture Book Studio, Simon & Schuster.

Day, A. 1995. *Carl goes to daycare.* New York: Farrar, Straus & Giroux.

Day, A. 1989. *Good dog, Carl.* New York: Simon & Schuster.

dePaola, T. 1978. *Pancakes for breakfast.* New York: Harcourt Brace Jovanovich.

Drescher, H. 1987. *The yellow umbrella.* New York: Bradbury.

Goodall, J.S. 1976. *The surprise picnic.* New York: Margaret K. McElderry.

Hutchins, P. 1971. *Changes.* New York: Macmillan.

Kitchen, B. 1984. *Animal alphabet.* New York: Dial.

Krahn, F. 1985. *Amanda and the mysterious carpet.* New York: Clarion.

McCully, E.A. 1987. *School.* New York: Harper & Row.

MacGregor, M. 1988. *On top.* New York: Morrow.

Mayer, M., & M. Mayer. 1975. *One frog too many.* New York: Dial.

Ormerod, J. 1982. *Moonlight.* New York: Lothrop, Lee & Shepard

Ormerod, J. 1981. *Sunshine.* New York: Lothrop, Lee & Shepard.

Prater, J. 1985. *The gift.* New York: Viking Kestrel.

Schories, P. 1991. *Mouse around.* New York: Farrar, Straus & Giroux.

Smith, L. 1988. *Flying Jake.* New York: Macmillan.

Spier, P. 1997. *Peter Spier's rain.* New York: Doubleday.

Spier, P. 1986. *Dreams.* New York: Doubleday.

Tafuri, N. 1994. *This is the farmer.* New York: Greenwillow.

Tafuri, N. 1990. *Junglewalk.* New York: Greenwillow.

Turkle, B. 1992. *Deep in the forest.* New York: Dutton.

Adapted from Reese, C. 1996. Story development using wordless picture books. *The Reading Teacher* (50): 172–73.

Songs and Fingerplays

Songs and chants offer endless opportunities for children to enjoy and explore language. Besides stretching their vocabulary and sound awareness as they sing well-loved songs, you can multiply the fun and learning by engaging children in playing with songs' words and sounds. For example, make a substitution in a familiar song or chant (such as, "The cow jumped over the house") and invite the children to come up with a new rhyme ("And the dish ran away with the mouse").

Suggestions for Helping English-Language Learners

• Use multimedia such as videos, pictures, and concrete objects to create connections with vocabulary words.

• Use gestures and body language.

• Speak slowly, and enunciate clearly. Do not raise your voice.

• Repeat information and review. If a child does not understand, try rephrasing in short sentences and simpler syntax.

• Try to avoid idioms and slang words.

• Try to anticipate words that might be unfamiliar and give explicit meaning to them.

• Make use of the excellent language learning that occurs among children by supporting play and small-group activities.

• Show children how much you enjoy them and appreciate their efforts to learn a new language.

Adapted from Cecil, N.L. 1999. *Striking a balance: Positive practices for early literacy.* Scottsdale, AZ: Holcomb Hathaway.

To comprehend what they read, children must continually draw on relevant background knowledge. This means that having a solid conceptual and informational base is a vital part of becoming a skilled reader. Thus a key curriculum goal in early childhood programs must be promoting children's acquisition of knowledge, concepts, and vocabulary.

Unfortunately, many children come to early childhood programs with a knowledge base that is quite narrow or may be mismatched to the content encountered in school. With these children, early childhood teachers have even more work to do. From the first day, they and the children must play catch-up.

Toddlers and preschoolers are able to learn new words at a phenomenal rate, provided they are in a language-rich setting in which adults read and talk with them and in which they are able to talk and play with other children. To develop basic concepts about objects and events, young children need opportunities to explore, manipulate, sort, and use materials in a variety of ways.

Young children need to be exposed to information books and other nonfiction as well as storybooks. Teachers should consider the *content* of both nonfiction and fiction text, keeping in mind how it connects to the curriculum and builds on what children already know.

Teachers can help children link new information and ideas to what they already understand. Useful strategies include

• *asking questions* that encourage children to notice, compare, and put things together ("Have you ever seen an animal that looks like this?");

• *making use of similarities and connections* in giving children new information ("Marmosets are in the monkey family, but they're smaller than the monkeys we saw at the zoo"); and

• *encouraging children to recollect and apply past experience* to a new situation ("Let's think about what our ant colony did when the weather got colder").

Children's knowledge grows through field trips and classroom visitors. But this learning is maximized when teachers lay the groundwork beforehand. Reading children a relevant book or showing them a video enables children to construct preliminary ideas about what a place is like and what goes on there. And by giving children some vocabulary and information in advance—on the ways of polar bears, for instance— we usually heighten their attentiveness during the trip. We can invite children to predict what they will be seeing and hearing, record their ideas for them or have them do so, and revisit these ideas on return.

Children encounter new concepts, information, and vocabulary through books and other media, outings and errands with their families, class field trips. But it is through their own subsequent activities, such as projects and play, that they explore and assimilate their new learning. Children experiment and share the fragments of information and limited understandings that each has gleaned, fitting them together and making the knowledge their own.

When children write, draw, dictate, build, dramatize, or through any such mode represent what they know and experience, they actively construct, internalize, and refine knowledge and concepts. Moreover, their visible productions allow teachers to see what children understand and what misconceptions they have.

Learning More about . . . Anything!

Children are naturally curious about the world around them. Bugs and birds, snakes and sharks, coins and cars, all of these and more can fascinate young children. Teachers and parents, recognizing what appeals to a particular child at a certain point in time, can work together in and out of school to build upon that child's budding interest. And if we as educators can help parents to be more comfortable and adept at this, children's ongoing learning— and the family's fun—will be enhanced year after year.

Here are some basic guidelines to share with parents:

• **Don't overdo and don't take over.** Helping a child to expand on his interest does *not* mean setting out to create the world's youngest expert in reptiles or volcanoes. Start small. Share a few books relating to the topic. Talk with the child about what he finds most interesting about whatever has captured his imagination. Ask him what he wants to know about it. Does he wonder where birds go when it rains? Why snails hide in their shells? How rocks get their color?

• **Help the child learn where to go next.** Write down a list of the child's questions about the topic, then research and explore together at the library. You can begin by looking in encyclopedias or on the Internet. Or bring the list to the children's librarian, who may be able to point out some children's books about your child's favorite subject.

• **Look for ways to give your child a greater range of experiences with the things that fascinate her.** If she's interested in bugs, go on an insect safari with magnifying glasses, a field book to help identify what you see, and a collection box to bring a few bugs home for further observation. Rocks, shells, feathers, flowers— children can hunt them all in the same way. For less house-friendly interests, such as snakes or polar bears, you can take a trip to the zoo, which may offer special learning programs for children. Museums, planetariums, and aquariums are also great places to go exploring with kids.

• **Let the child's interest evolve in its own direction.** Don't become locked into keeping the focus on the original point of departure. If a trip to the aquarium shifts the child's love of goldfish into a burning desire for all things octopus, be ready to make another trip to the library to get more books and investigate a new list of questions. Every now and then, add a few questions of your own to that list; it shows the child that you don't know all the answers either and that you too enjoy learning new things.

Making New Words and Concepts Meaningful

If you introduce new concepts and vocabulary effectively, they are more likely to stick. Some basic guidelines:

• **Begin with what children already know.** Instead of telling children the meaning of words or concepts they may not know, ask them, "What do you know about these words?" It is never too early to begin encouraging children to take risks by guessing and hypothesizing about new words based upon what they do know.

• **Use as many senses as possible when introducing new words and concepts.** *Telling* children the meanings of new words may not be particularly effective. Action words can be acted out by the class ("*Show* me exhausted!"); other words can be sung, drawn, or demonstrated ("This is how you pirouette!"). And don't forget the old saying, also true in vocabulary acquisition, that a picture is worth a thousand words.

• **Give children meaningful opportunities to use their new words.** Just defining or demonstrating new words does not markedly increase vocabulary unless children actually use the words introduced. When words are used in daily conversations and activities, they are far more likely to become part of children's permanent vocabulary. Some teachers make use of direct strategies, such as challenging children to look for chances to use a new word in the course of the day or week, then recording their sentences and sharing them with the whole group. Asking questions (open-ended or giving limited choices) to provoke children's use of new words is another effective strategy. ("This lemon doesn't taste sweet like the orange—it's kind of sour. How does your lime taste, Timothy?")

• **Model curiosity about words and good dictionary habits.** An excellent preliminary introduction to the dictionary habit for children not yet ready to use one is to observe a respected adult musing, "I wonder what that word means?" and then looking it up and sharing the meaning with the class.

Adapted from Cecil, N.L. 1999. *Striking a balance: Positive practices for early literacy.* Scottsdale, AZ: Holcomb Hathaway.

Print is part of children's world virtually from the beginning, though at first it holds little interest for them. Infants respond to language and enjoy looking at picture books and being read to. As for print itself, there are far more exciting things to investigate.

Yet by age two or three, children begin to develop a degree of print awareness as they experience people around them reading, writing, and using the printed word for many purposes.

5 animal crackers

1 cup juice

SAVE SIN DANIEL

We enhance children's awareness that print conveys meaning when we make comments like these:

"We have to wait here. That sign says, 'Don't walk.'"

"I'm writing 'Adam' on your painting so everyone will know whose it is."

"Everybody, check snack menu to see how many animal crackers you can have."

"If you want to work more on this tower tomorrow, we'll make a 'Save' sign to let the afternoon class know."

Children love to recognize, and later to write, their own names. And long before they go to school, young children can learn to spot letters important to them, such as the *S* of *Sesame Street* or the *z* of *zoo,* and begin to notice the general shape and length of familiar words.

Encourage preschoolers to figure out the meaning of the print they see—on a sign or a T-shirt or in a greeting card, magazine, or book—using their repertoire of known letters and cues such as word length. Challenge them to make educated guesses—to be "print detectives."

"Can anyone tell me which of the words on our shopping list is *juice*?"

"Nolan isn't here today. Can you find me his folder, Jeanne?"

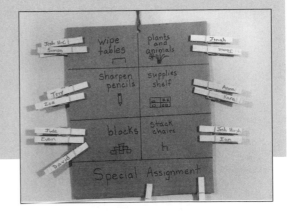

As we read, write, and play with children, assisting them in their enterprises and sharing with them knowledge about the world they live in, we have many opportunities to help them learn how print works. We read the book title and author name whenever we begin to read a book aloud. Occasionally we point out a particular word, like *Pooh* or *zebra*. Running a finger along the text from time to time shows children that we read from left to right and from top to bottom on the page.

Without adults drawing attention to paragraph breaks, punctuation, lowercase and uppercase letters, and other such features of text, children typically do not give them much notice. With preschool and kindergarten children, teachers may begin mentioning these print features in reading aloud, taking dictation, or assisting children in their own reading or writing efforts. By saying "Let me finish this sentence before we talk about that question," or "I'll start a new paragraph for this part where you start home from the beach," the teacher highlights the sentence or paragraph as a meaningful unit.

In the primary grades teachers will provide more explicit instruction on such mechanics and encourage children to note them in reading and use them in writing, especially in preparing final drafts.

The Camera Project

While brainstorming creative ways for second-graders to develop their writing skills and vocabulary, Michael Savage, Derek Holcomb, and the student teachers whom they supervised came up with this project. Through photographs from home or, better still, pictures they take themselves, children can share with peers and teachers their favorite things and the familiar people and events of home.

Start by familiarizing the children with simple cameras. Some children may have used a camera and can contribute what they know about taking pictures. Review how to open and load the camera, frame a shot through the view finder, keep thumbs away from the lens, and push the button to take the picture. Allow children in small groups to explore an empty camera.

Once the children are comfortable with cameras, send a note to parents explaining the project, along with a camera and photo log sheet. Encourage parents to talk with their children about possible subjects they could photograph—a neighborhood friend or family member, a special spot at home, a favorite toy. Ask parents to accompany their child on their photo shoot, jotting down on the photo log what the child dictates about each shot. When the roll is finished, parents should label it with their child's name and return it to the classroom with the camera and their photo log.

After the film has been developed, be sure to label every shot in pencil with the photographer's name before passing out prints. For the young photographers, getting their photos back is a very exciting moment! Allow sufficient time for the children to go through their shots and share them with one another.

When the children have had time to go through their photographs, they are ready to write or dictate text to go with the pictures. You might lay the groundwork by reading a book with photographs, engaging children in noticing how photos *help* to tell the story and provide information but are not enough to communicate everything the author wants the reader to know. Demonstrate this by looking at some of the children's shots and making wild guesses about what is happening in the picture. When children correct you ("No, that wasn't what happened!"), they are primed to write or dictate what they want others to know about their pictured events, people, or places. In a small way they are becoming more aware that we must consider our audiences when we write.

Working with children individually or in groups of two or three, encourage them to write stories or other text using their pictures as a springboard. Here too, remind them that their books will be looked at by others—teachers, other children—who weren't with them when they took the photos. As the stories or "photo essays" take shape, the pictures and strips of accompanying text can be glued to sheets of construction paper, then stapled together as books. The children can read their books to classmates and take them home to share with family members.

For complete details on this project, see Savage, M.P., & D.R. Holcomb. 1999. Children, cameras, and challenging projects. *Young Children* 54 (2): 27–29.

Signs and Logos

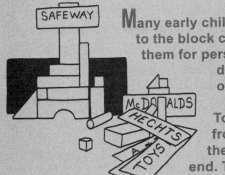

Many early childhood programs have commercial traffic signs added to the block corner. Although children do enjoy these and may use them for personal means, they are somewhat limiting, as they deal solely with traffic movement. One teacher felt that other forms of signs would enhance her block area. The teacher cuts logos for local stores—McDonald's, Toys'R Us, Superfresh Supermarket, Eckerd's Drugs—from advertisements and shopping bags. She attached the logos with masking tape to unit blocks stood on end. These were then spread along the top of the block shelf. The teacher said nothing about the signs. When the children came in, they immediately began building stores to go with the signs. The signs added a prompt to suggest what could be built.

When a needed sign was being used by someone else, some of the children copied the sign. Others searched through a collection of paper bags for another logo they could cut out and use. With an older class, the teacher might have involved the children in finding logos and making the original signs. If extra unit blocks are not available, the logos can be attached to toilet paper rolls, empty salt containers, or small boxes filled with newspaper to weigh them down.

Adapted with permission from Davidson, J. 1996. *Emerging literacy and dramatic play in early education.* Albany, NY: Delmar.

The Daily Menu

Seeing a menu of snack or lunch gives children a meaningful experience—what is more meaningful than food?—with letters, words, and getting information from print. On menus for younger children and English-language learners, include pictures or photographs of the food items next to the words. Consulting the menu becomes a daily habit, and some children begin to recognize simple words and name single letters. For older children use print-only menus, or try an in-between version in which children try to identify each item from print alone but then can open a flap to look at the picture and see if they were right.

To support children's print awareness, try strategies like these:

• Show children the menu with only words visible and invite them to predict the snack for the day, emphasizing how the written words provide this information.

• Ask the child or group of children what they notice about the words or letters being examined. For instance, "How many words do you see here for this food?"

• Whatever the child's level, your interactions can help. For example, when a child knows some letters and is beginning to grasp that the letters in the printed word correspond to the sounds in the spoken word, you can say something like, "Here's how I know this word might be *peanut.* It starts with a *p,* and that says /p/."

• Ask children to think of other foods they might like to have for snack that begin with the same letter or sound.

• Use menus to talk to the children about the types of foods that keep them strong and healthy.

Children also enjoy making their own menus to use in playing restaurant or perhaps to take home to show their parents what they ate that day. You can give them copies of the printed menu and suggest they draw the food items or cut out pictures from old magazines. Or you can provide picture menus on which children write the food names, writing at whatever level each is able to manage.

When adults read to children regularly, children's familiarity with stories and other kinds of text begins to evolve well before they are able to read or write. From such experience, children learn to distinguish the language used in books from conversational language and to anticipate certain elements in a story. Later, these expectations assist children in comprehending what they read and in creating their own compositions.

Once upon a time there were three children who lived in a cottage on the edge of a large wood. The eldest . . .

Hearing a story read again and again, children are better able to put together the relation of the characters and the sequence of key events, which they often fail to do on a first reading. Repeated readings thus enhance children's awareness of basic narrative elements. Asking a child to retell a story in his own words allows the teacher to determine the child's understanding and his familiarity with story elements and structure.

In dramatic play children create and enact stories. These experiences stand them in good stead when reading and composing narratives. As children pretend, they talk about what is happening—setting the scene, managing and adjusting the roles and action, bridging over parts they cannot easily act out. Knowing little of what his parents do at work, for example, a child says, "The dad went to work and now he's home." Supplying such narrative language about events, characters, and settings prepares children to read and write stories.

Young children are just learning to take account of the listener's needs in conversation. But they find it very difficult to put in writing what a reader may need to understand their meaning. To help with this learning, we can pose questions or make comments as children dictate or as we read back their compositions ("When you say in your instructions, *pull it,* do you mean the handle or the lever?").

Because peer comments and questions heighten children's awareness of the audience's understanding, another useful strategy is having children write in pairs or groups.

Dramatizing stories connects children's love of pretend play to more formal storytelling. As children act out favorite stories, songs, and poetry, as well as stories they have created themselves, they develop narrative skills.

In collaborating to enact stories or enjoying them as audience members, children develop knowledge about how to begin and end a story, how to use narrator commentary and character dialogue, and how to employ other elements of effective storytelling.

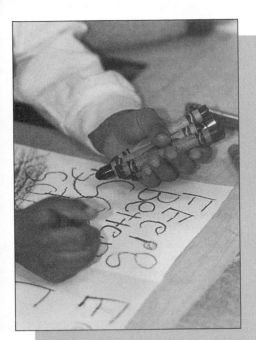

Besides reading stories, we can acquaint young children with other written forms: poems, letters, lists, notices, invitations, even advertisements and comic strips. Sometimes teachers may demonstrate how to write in a new genre, but children most effectively learn about a form of writing when they have a real purpose for using it.

There are many things we can do to kindle children's interest in new text forms and formats. For example, a teacher may suggest writing a note to a sick friend or making a poster to announce a coming event. Within ongoing projects or dramatic play, we can also look for ways to engage children in various kinds of writing that relate to what they are doing. For instance, one teacher took advantage of children's deep involvement in playing auto shop to introduce a wide variety of new genres that related to their play, as described on pages 76–79.

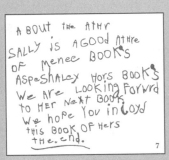

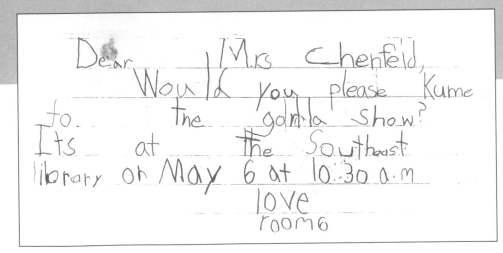

The Children's Garage

Dramatic play has the potential to powerfully enhance young children's literacy learning. Summarized here is a case study from Nigel Hall and Anne Robinson's book, *Exploring Writing and Play in the Early Years,* that illustrates many inventive ways in which a teacher uses play to enlarge children's writing repertoire. For the 12 weeks during which the children in Mrs. Booth's class "played garage," she found ways to help them learn about a wide variety of forms of writing and print (pp. 48–104).

At the outset Mrs. Booth made plans for her class of 4- and 5-year-olds to visit a local auto shop, Pipe's Garage. Before the trip she discussed with them what they might look for. Writing down their ideas on a chart, she also gave children clipboards to note what they saw on the trip.

Figure 2

At the garage, Mr. Pipe showed the children around and allowed them to handle various tools and watch the mechanics at work. He gave the children car parts and equipment to take back to school—a fan belt, spark plugs, jump leads, and switches.

Back in the classroom the children examined the garage items and discussed the many things that happen in garages and the jobs that are done. Play areas

Figure 1

related to a field trip in Mrs. Booth's class usually started up promptly after such a visit, but the children needed several days to build the garage and get it ready to open for business. To keep the children's interest high while construction was going on, and to acquaint them with aspects of how the real world works, Mrs. Booth devised a variety of relevant experiences involving writing such as

• drawing up plans for what the garage would look like,

• writing a letter to Town Hall to request permission to build (Figure 1), and

• filling out a planning application form sent in response to the children's letter.

Lists of stock for the garage were produced, as well as labels and signs (Figure 2), all relatively easy tasks for the less confident writers in the group. The children also

• created posters and announcements for the garage opening (Figures 3 and 5),

• wrote advertisements for jobs (Figure 4) and filled in job application forms (Figure 6),

Figure 3

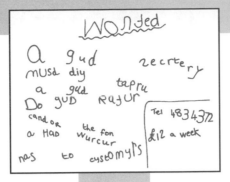

Figure 4

• created and wrote rules and instructions, and

• wrote a newspaper story and created ads for the garage.

Some of the reading and writing experiences evolved directly from the children as they played. In other cases Mrs. Booth created situations outside the play setting, but drawing on the power of the play, to engage the children in new challenges in reading, writing, and problem solving.

For example, Mrs. Booth arranged for the children to receive a letter of complaint from someone in the school office, expressing concern that the garage was likely to be noisy, dirty, and perhaps dangerous. Working out how to respond, composing a letter to reassure the writer, and waiting to see if their letter was effective—these experiences deeply engrossed the children for days.

They also received a letter from the younger class requesting repair of one of the school's tricycles. The children examined the trike and prepared a written estimate for needed repairs (Figure 7).

Later, questioned about the estimate being high, they wrote back explaining the reasons for the costs (Figure 8).

In another instance, this note arrived for Mrs. Booth's children:

> *Dear Class 3,*
>
> *I read in the newspaper that you have recently opened a garage. I have a friend who is blind and when I told her about your garage, she wanted to know more about it. I wonder whether some of you could write and describe your garage so I could read the letters to my friend. She would be very interested because she has never been to a garage.* (pp. 80–81)

At first the children's responses were general. That is, they proposed telling the lady that the garage had an office, a car-lift, and the like. The need to be descriptive in communicating, particularly with a person without sight and lacking experience of garages, was difficult for the children to grasp, much less to translate into specifics, as we see in the following exchange:

It wil biy clin and tadi and it wot biy horbl.
We wil wosh or haz biyfur wiy tuch yur cor.
We dw put the tooz away and we wot brc yor cors and we wot let the caz go fruw the rhf. Wiy wot smash wiz and wiy wot smash eny cars.

The peepol hep the nuv peepol. dey whrk hod. The ofis peepol or smaliy.

Hiy wud brus up with the brus and wosh or hans.

Figure 5

The Children's Garage

Teacher: This blind lady, can she see anything?

Child: She might have a dog.

Teacher: Well, she might. . . . Will the dog be able to tell her what [the car-lift is] like?

Child: The dog will be able to say 'Woof, woof.' (p. 81)

From such attempts Mrs. Booth decided the children needed more specific experience in describing before they could manage this demanding task. She introduced the game of describing an object to someone blindfolded, and then she had the children write descriptions of things found in a garage without mentioning the items' names. Eventually the class decided to make a "blind book" for the lady. They decided to put in the book actual samples of substances such as rubber and metal and to cut items of thick cardboard to enable the lady to identify shapes by touch.

Through these experiences the children got better at writing descriptions that considered the particular needs of the audience.

Figure 6

Figure 7

They wrote, for example, "The hammer has a long stick and the end is metal and the end is oblong. You bang nails with a hammer. It is nearly as big as my arm."

Throughout the months of garage play and related writing tasks, the children were intensely involved. And the girls were as interested as the boys in playing garage, perhaps because of the sustained nature of the activity and the remarkable variety of roles it opened up.

Clearly, the children in Mrs. Booth's class gained lots of writing and reading experience over this period. Even more striking than the quantity of their experience is the very rich array of text forms—many of them unusual in young children's experience—which ranged from writing job applications and advertisements to composing letters for various recipients and purposes. Hall and Robinson remark,

Far from putting the children off, these challenges were relished by the children. They had tremendous fun sorting them out and responding appropriately. They brought to the activities a sense of energy, and purpose. It is clearly the case that teachers should not avoid unusual types of writing but should view them as opportunities to develop an understanding of many complex events in the world (pp. 96–97).

Without the garage play, such writing activities would have been purposeless to the children—just another batch of teacher-imposed tasks. Instead, the writ-

FRom The maniC

mi pipepag Rage,
The MuD gaD Woz WoBLiY
The Sit it Woz WoBLiY
The Bac Woz SWiGn
The aguLBaz muVin
The pet Woz CUm uf
it nR noooyoL on it

it WiL COSD 44 Paz FoR FiSnit

Figure 8

ing tasks were meaningful and important. Hall and Robinson conclude,

Of course, teachers can provide direct experiences of writing in genres through exercises and demonstrations. But the experience of learning about a way of writing is much more significant and relevant when the demand seems necessary and relevant to the learner. Socio-dramatic play can make the experience of using and understanding of genres (or text forms) much easier (p. 47).

The truth of this statement is evident in the great variety of forms in which children wrote during their garage days and in the eager intensity they brought to these tasks.

Nigel Hall and Anne Robinson described the children's garage in a case study in *Exploring Writing and Play in the Early Years*, London: David Fulton Publishers, 1995. Samples of children's work and quoted material used with permission.

Book Backpacks

Send home book backpacks to introduce quality children's literature into children's homes and to engage parents and kids together in beginning literacy experiences. To assemble a book backpack, start by choosing five to seven quality children's books centered on a theme, author, genre or a child's special interest. You may want to include a letter to parents or a brochure on what goes on in your classroom to promote literacy. Also include a response notebook for children to write about the books in the backpack and an inventory card listing the backpack's contents.

To get the book backpack program started, send home a letter that describes the program. Tell parents that backpacks go home on Thursday and should be returned by the following Thursday. This time frame gives working parents plenty of time to read and reread the books with their children.

Make a list to record the children's names, the particular backpacks they choose, and the dates the backpacks will be returned. To help keep track of stray books that do not make it back to school, ask parent volunteers to spend an hour each week checking the backpacks' contents.

Lynn E. Cohen, a kindergarten teacher in Great Neck, New York, developed the book backpack program. For a detailed description of how to fund, establish, and manage a book backpack program, see Cohen, L.A. 1997. How I developed my kindergarten book backpack program, *Young Children* 52 (2): 69–71.

Starting in infancy children become increasingly sensitive to the sounds of speech. Babies and toddlers enjoy hearing songs, rhymes, and chants. Their babbling goes through a gradual shift to include more and more the speech sounds they hear around them.

Learning to read requires that children have considerable awareness of the sound structure of spoken language. Thus, not only kindergarten and primary-grade teachers but also teachers of younger children must give careful attention to children's development of phonological awareness.

Gina (2 years): *Dilly milly, dolly molly, silly dilly, silly dolly.* (plays with sounds while being bathed)

Few young children spontaneously acquire phonemic awareness. But when teachers plan activities and interact so as to draw attention to the phonemes in spoken words, children's awareness develops.

We can add a dimension of phonological awareness to common classroom routines such as attendance taking and transitions from one activity to the next. For instance, when it's time for children to leave the circle and go to a center of their choice, the teacher might say, "First, everyone whose name starts with the same sound as *red* and *run* . . . "

Many children's stories and poems are full of rhymes, alliteration, and lively play with the sounds of language. When predictable rhythms and rhyme patterns are present, as in *The Cat in the Hat* and *Fox in Socks* by Dr. Seuss, children often are able to supply a rhyming word to complete the line, and they may go on to make up their own silly rhymes and verses.

"Chicks with bricks come.
Chicks with blocks come.
Chicks with bricks and blocks and clocks come."

— Dr. Seuss
from *Fox in Socks*

Hearing repeated readings of the same text also allows children to notice sound patterns. And when teachers make sure the page is clearly visible, sometimes pointing to words as they read, children begin to pick up letter-sound relationships.

Teachers promote phonological awareness and letter-sound connections when they provide frequent opportunity and reasons for children to write on their own. As children work out how to write something down, they focus on the sounds that make up words. At first their writing tends to look like P G L D because they pick up only the initial sounds of words. Over time children begin to add middle and final sounds.

When a child seeks help in writing a word, the teacher may try saying the word slowly, emphasizing each sound. Or she may make a comment such as, "*Butter?* Sounds as if it starts with the same sound as your name, Bonita." When a child clearly wants the conventional spelling, the teacher can simply provide it or perhaps suggest where to find it ("If you're trying to write *Monday*, you could check the calendar").

iSTnD no Sn.

"I stand in the sun."

THe DES BLOJ THe

CIT N THe R

"The wind is blowing the kite in the air."

		six	doctor	view	yellow	zero
Tom	Oct.	sics	dacr	vivd	yeitto	zro
	Mar.	siz	docdr	vuooe	yelleo	zuro
	June	six	docker	vuoo	ywello	zero
Emily	Oct.	sis	docdil	vow	yollew	zero
	Mar.	six	docdr	vuoe	yellow	zero
	June	six	docder	vyou	yellow	zero
Bobby	Oct.	sies	dacdr	vquow	yellow	sero
	Mar.	sicks	daktr	vyou	yilloo	ziro
	June	sixs	daktor	vuow	yellow	zero
Kevin	Oct.	ses	ditr	veu	eelo	sero
	Mar.	segs	dgd	foyou	ylo	zero
	June	six	dokdr	vaue	yalo	zeroe

From Armington, D. 1997. *The living classroom: Writing, reading, and beyond*, p. 31. Washington, DC: NAEYC

Singing rhyming chants and songs, clapping or tapping out the syllables of words—these simple activities heighten preschoolers' attention to the sounds of speech. Teachers can also devise games and activities that encourage older preschoolers and kindergartners to sort words into word families, such as *cat*, *hat*, and *bat* (*rimes*), or to group them by their beginning sounds (known as *onsets*).

Getting the *p*-words straight

Phonological awareness refers to the whole spectrum from primitive awareness of speech sounds and rhythms to rhyme awareness and sound similarities and, at the highest level, awareness of syllables or phonemes. *Phonemes* are the smallest units in speech, for instance, the /b/, /a/, and /t/ sounds that make up the word *bat*.

Becoming attentive to the sound structure of language—becoming phonologically or phonemically aware—is an "ear" skill, unlike *phonics*, which is the relation between letters and sounds in written words.

ick	ink	ing
sick	sink	king
kick	stink	sing
pick	think	thing
tick		singing
lick		wing
click		
stick		

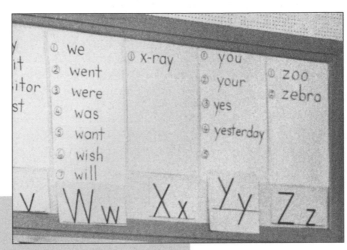

Besides continuing to use the full range of teaching strategies effective in the preschool years, teachers boost the phonological awareness of kindergarten and primary-grade children by inviting them to

- build word walls, emphasizing common sounds they hear;

- isolate the first segment of a word ("Can you say the first little bit of *snow*?");

- find all the things in a picture that begin with the /n/ sound; and

- tell what is left when one of the segments is removed from a word ("Say *smile* without the 'sss'" or "Say *team* without the 'mmm'") (Burns, Griffin, & Snow 1999)

Developmental Spellings

Developmental spellings, sometimes called invented spellings, are the early spellings that children produce independently. They result from children's experimentations with writing and their developing knowledge of language and its sounds.

• There are some general patterns to children's spelling and writing development. Scribbling often represents children's first efforts to communicate through writing. They frequently talk while scribbling, demonstrating their understanding that symbols written on paper have meaning.

• Children progress from scribbling to one-letter spelling. They frequently use the initial consonant in their name or in some other distinctive word, such as *M* for *mom*. As they continue to experiment with spelling, they add other distinctive consonants, along with other groupings of letters such as *trz* for *trees*. Vowels are usually added much later than consonants. As children work to produce developmental spellings, they are listening to the sounds in the words and increasingly learning how these sounds are written—an extremely valuable process for readers in the making.

• Children eventually begin to write two and three word phrases as they develop simple rules. Again, their rules may not yet conform with our rules, but they demonstrate a growing understanding of the patterns in language.

To make good use of children's evolving spellings in their learning to read and write, keep in mind some guidelines:

• **Don't expect immediate correctness in young children's spelling.** Their spellings will become more standard as they write and read and as they learn more about spelling patterns. In the meantime, they are learning to enjoy writing and to feel they can do it on their own. By contrast, worrying about making a spelling error and feeling dependent on the adult to supply all spellings inhibits children's engagement in writing and that active listening for the sounds in words that is so useful for budding readers.

• **Look for opportunities to talk about writing.** For example, when you write a caption on a child's picture, you might ask, "What letters should I write for this picture?" or say, "You can write about your picture—what letters do you need?" (Remember never to write directly on their work, but at the bottom of the page or on a separate strip). Such questions enhance children's phonemic awareness as they attempt to write down the letters that they can hear in words.

• **Encourage children to read their "writing" before you try to interpret it.** You might say, "Can you read your writing to me?" Using the term *writing* rather than *drawing* helps children begin to think of themselves as writers. If they choose not to read it, then you might point out some of the interesting features that you see in their writing.

• **Don't make developmental spelling an end in itself.** When a child asks you to spell a word for him, he shows his awareness that a "right" spelling exists—and he wants to know what it is. This is not the time to say, "What do you think?" Whenever possible write the whole word on a card. Seeing the word in its entirety, rather than hearing individual letter names being spelled aloud, helps the child form a visual picture of the word and its configuration.

The flower in California is orange. It is very very pretty

Sound-tration

Modeled after the game Concentration, this activity helps children become aware of the initial phonemes in words. Using pictures of familiar objects, they get experience in comparing beginning sounds.

Gather pictures of familiar objects that begin with the same sound, and mount them on cards. During circle time, spread a few pictures out where children

can see them. Make sure that the objects start with a simple initial sound such as /b/ or /s/ and not a more complex sound like /fr/ (known as a consonant blend) or /ch/ or /sh/ (known as a digraph).

Begin the game by asking the children to find a picture that starts with the same sound as the one you hold up. When they find the picture, children say the word. They take turns until all the cards have been matched.

In smaller groups, let each child take a turn flipping any two pictures face up and deciding if the initial sounds of the pictures' names are the same. If the initial sounds match, the child keeps the pair and gets to try again; otherwise the next child takes a turn.

To vary the activity, use picture cards with rhyming words. It's a fun way for children to become familiar with word families (*cat, bat, hat, rat*), which will eventually be useful for decoding activities.

This activity and dozens of others are described on http://www.ed.gov/Family/RWN/Activ97/, the Website of America Reads Challenge READ*WRITE*NOW!

Letters and words are the basic building blocks of print. To read, children must be able to distinguish the letters of the alphabet and to connect letters and letter clusters with sounds. To become proficient readers they need to be able to recognize many familiar words at a glance as well as decode words they don't know by sight.

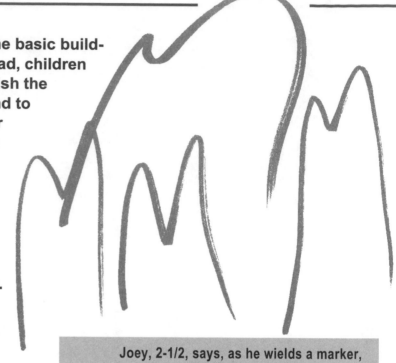

Joey, 2-1/2, says, as he wields a marker, "This McDonald's." Then he says, "This Mama."

"That's my name!" says 3-year-old Sasha, spying a stop sign. Although she doesn't yet know all the letters of her name, she recognizes the familiar *S* from the many times grownups have pointed out her name to her. Sasha is now able to spot the letter just about anywhere it appears, even though it takes on many faces—S, *s*, S, S, and so on.

While lots of preschoolers know a letter or two that appear in their names, that is often the extent of their experience with letters and words. And children whose parents haven't pointed

out letters or words in print are likely to have very limited letter knowledge when they first enter an early childhood setting. For this reason, over the preschool and kindergarten years we want to expand all children's familiarity with print, including individual letters, and help them begin to notice letter/sound connections.

By the end of kindergarten, children should be able to readily recognize and name the letters of the alphabet, whether in lowercase or uppercase. To enable them to do so, we give them extensive experiences with letters throughout the preschool and kindergarten years. Reading alphabet books with children and making alphabet books together are helpful. And there are many other ways to make letters an integral part of the classroom environment and curriculum.

Where are the letters in a developmentally appropriate, literacy-promoting classroom?

• Where children can see them

Alphabet displays way above children's heads are of little use. Letters need to be at eye level where children can examine them.

• Where children can refer to them as they work and play

When they are writing, children are far more likely to make use of letter guides that are close at hand. Teachers can apply alphabet strips to tabletops (Davidson 1996) or laminate letter-writing guides that children can take off a shelf or peg and bring with them to wherever they are writing (Schickedanz 1999).

• Where children can handle them

Children notice the shapes of letters when they do alphabet puzzles or use letter-shaped cookie cutters in damp sand or dough. Magnetic letters and alphabet blocks allow children to explore letter/sound connections, arrange and rearrange letters to form words, and become more aware of the sequences of sounds within words.

All children need some direct help with letter/sound patterns and decoding skills. But such help is usually most effective not in isolated lessons but within the context of meaningful reading experiences, taking children's dictation and reading it back, and supporting them in their efforts to read and write.

A useful habit for teachers to develop is talking about letters and sounds as they write messages to children or help them compose written products. For example, a teacher may say, "This sentence has several words starting with *b*, that sound we hear in *bear*, *baby*, and *boy*. Let's read that again . . . " and point to each *b* as she reads the word.

Readers and Writers in the Making

When children in their attempts at writing show that they realize letters represent sounds, teachers can start helping them individually to write the sounds they hear in words. And as their sounded-out spellings evolve, teachers help children make the transition to conventional spellings.

Child: Did I spell *today* right?

Teacher: T-O-D-A, you have all the sounds. Just add a *y* at the end and you'll have it. *Day, say, hay,* all those words have the *ay.*

Readers and Writers in the Making

One of the best ways to help children learn letter/ sound relations is to draw their attention to initial word sounds known as *onsets* (such as *p-* in *pie* or *bl-* in *black*) and word endings, or *rimes* (such as *–ake*, *-ent*, and *–ish*). We can do this as we read and reread stories and verses rich in alliteration and rhyming. We may explicitly draw children's attention to such patterns while reading or writing with them. When working with first-graders or kindergartners (and occasionally inter-ested preschoolers), we can involve children in making word lists, word banks, or books of words that share interesting spelling/sound patterns.

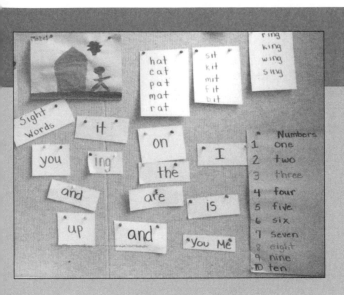

Teachers boost children's reading fluency through word-directed activities that help them acquire a basic sight vocabulary. Especially important for children to recognize automatically are frequently appearing words such as *said* or *they*. Freed from having to sound out every word, children will more easily grasp and keep track of the meaning of text. Among the experiences that promote children's word recognition are engaging in building word walls, guessing mystery words, and seeing highlighted occurrences of the same word throughout a passage.

What can we do at the park?
We can slide down the slide.
We can dig in the sandbox. We
can swing on the swings. We
can climb up and down on the
bars.

Songs in Print

Songs promote language development and focus attention on rhymes and other sound patterns. They are also a wonderful way to help children connect words and meaning with print. Choose a song illustrated in a picture book, preferably a Big Book. Read the book aloud several times, inviting the children to join in singing or saying the words of the song.

Link the song to print by displaying the lyrics on a chart, inviting the children to read along—and then sing along—as you point to each word in the song. Here are some other ways to extend and reinforce the connections of words and print.

♪ Send home the lyrics of this song, as well as other songs and fingerplays children learn at school, for parents to sing with them at home. As we all know, kids love teaching their parents something new!

♪ Place the song picture book in the listening area, along with an audiotape of the book being read on one side and sung on the other.

♪ Challenge children to hunt for things on the song chart, for example, words that appear more than once, words that rhyme or begin with a certain letter, or words in a certain category, such as animal sounds in *Old MacDonald Had a Farm* or the various people who appear in *The Wheels on the Bus*.

♪ On a pocket chart of the song, invite children to insert the missing phrases, which are written out on sentence strips. Place the original song nearby for the children to consult if they wish. They'll learn a lot even when they're playing with mixing up phrases and laughing at the results, such as chicks making "a moo-moo here and a moo-moo there."

♪ In songs with repeating phrases, such as "Have you ever seen a . . . " in "Down by the Bay," highlight the phrase by writing it in a different color from the rest of the song. Also print the phrase at the top of a blank chart page and ask the children to supply new words, phrases, or perhaps names ("Have you ever seen Sam eating a ham?"), which you then write on the chart.

♪ Create a Big Book based on the song lyrics. Invite the children to dictate or write new lyrics that fit the song's repetitive pattern; some may want to illustrate the verses on large pieces of chart paper. Their illustrations and lyrics can be displayed on the wall and used for "read the wall" activities. After a week or so, take down the pages and bind them into a Big Book for the children to reread or take home to share with family members.

Kathy Barclay, an associate professor at Western Illinois University, and reading teacher Lynn Walwer wrote about these classroom-tested ideas for using songs to promote language development. For more information on using song picture books, see Barclay, K.D., & L. Walwer. 1992. Linking lyrics through song picture books. *Young Children* 47 (4): 76–85.

Learning Letters

Young children love to look at photographs of themselves and their friends. By displaying snapshots of every child in your class and having children match up faces to names, you can create an activity that provides experience in letter recognition and naming and in noticing the initial sound (phoneme) in a name.

On each poster attach four or five photographs, making sure to group together names beginning with the same letter. In the space to the right of each photo, draw a straight horizontal line. Laminate the boards, and then put a dot of Velcro on each line. Attach another dot of Velcro to the back of laminated tagboard name tags. Put the name tags that correspond to each set of photos in a small container, and place the container and its matching picture board on a classroom shelf with other matching/puzzle materials.

When children first use the materials, they won't know which name is which. You can help children identify a picture by saying, "We need to find the name that starts with *M*, for Mmmmichaela's picture. Let's see. This name starts with *B*, not *M*. This one. . . . What does it start with?" (Child answers *M*) "Yes it does! But you know what? That word does not say *Michaela*. It says *Matt*. Matt's name starts with *M*, but it ends with /ttt/. Let's see. This next one starts with *M*, and it says *Mmmmichaela*."

The photo-to-name matching activity can be used in a variety of ways. Each child can sign in on arrival by placing her name next to her photo. Or at circle time the child with the job of taking attendance for the day can make as many matches as he is able and then get help from the other children. The exercise can also be used in the puzzle area as an activity children can do on their own or with friends.

Adapted from Neuman, S.B., & K.A. Roskos, eds. 1998. *Children achieving: Best practices in early literacy.* Newark, DE: International Reading Association.

What's in a Word?

Using this simple read-aloud activity, you can highlight for children how the sequence of letters in a written word corresponds to the sequence of sounds they hear when the word is spoken.

Begin by writing a word that begins with a consonant. Ask the children to say the word. Now swap the initial consonant with another consonant and ask them to say the new word. Demonstrate the sounding and blending of the letters for them. After they have mastered swapping the initial consonant, try replacing the final consonants. When children are able to do this, try them on the harder task of switching the vowel sounds.

Initial consonant swap:	bat, cat, hat, mat, pat, sat, vat
Final consonant swap:	fit, fin, fib, fig
Vowel sound:	pat, pet, pit, pot *or* bit, bet, but

Taking Stock

of what you do to promote literacy

The preceding pages describe many developmentally appropriate practices proven effective in promoting children's proficiency and enthusiasm as readers and writers. This inventory is provided to help each of us to take stock, to examine our curriculum and classroom and consider whether we're doing everything we can to help children learn to read and write. Clearly, teaching practices should be varied according to the ages and developmental levels of the learners, and this brief overview could not capture that level of detail. (For more information and guidance in teaching a given age group, see Resources, pp. 127–130). The practices and strategies listed in the Taking Stock inventory are useful throughout the preschool and early grades.

THE POWER AND PLEASURE OF LITERACY

Do you . . .

- [ ] Read daily to children in your class?

- [ ] Engage children in selecting favorite books and participating actively in storytime?

- [ ] Find ways to encourage parents to read to their children at home?

- [ ] Link books and reading experiences with engaging activities that stretch children's learning?

- [ ] Show children the many ways that reading and writing can be used in daily activities?

- [ ] Include literacy props and materials in dramatic play areas?

THE LITERATE ENVIRONMENT

Do you . . .

- [ ] Put labels, captions, and other print in places where they serve a purpose?

- [ ] Create inviting places for children to read with their friends or on their own?

- [ ] Include a wide variety of books and print materials that affirm children's cultures and linguistic backgrounds?

- [ ] Place books where children can easily reach them?

- [ ] Display books on open shelves to pique children's interest in reading?

- [ ] Rotate and refresh literacy materials in dramatic play areas to keep children's interest and imaginations lively?

LANGUAGE DEVELOPMENT

Do you . . .

☐ Respond to what children do and say by building on their ideas and language?

☐ Include new words in your conversations with children?

☐ Name objects and actions, giving children a brief explanation where necessary?

☐ Engage children in language games, rhymes, and riddles?

☐ Encourage dramatic play and sometimes join in to introduce new possibilities?

☐ Create opportunities for children to engage in interactive activities in small groups?

BUILDING KNOWLEDGE AND COMPREHENSION

Do you . . .

☐ Give children many opportunities to explore and manipulate objects?

☐ Read and make available information books and other nonfiction?

☐ Introduce new vocabulary and concepts before going on special field trips?

☐ Debrief and discuss with children what they have learned after a field trip or other special activity?

☐ Ensure that there are abundant opportunities for children to share and assimilate knowledge through play?

☐ Ask children questions and respond to their questions?

☐ Identify and explain new words across the curriculum?

KNOWLEDGE OF PRINT

Do you . . .

☐ Show children that we read print moving from left to right and top to bottom?

☐ Identify the features of a book, such as the author and title?

☐ Point to words, labels, and letters and read or name them?

☐ Help children to recognize and write their names?

☐ Draw attention to uppercase and lowercase letters, punctuation, and other print features?

TYPES OF TEXT

Do you . . .

☐ Read and reread stories to give children a chance to become very familiar with them?

☐ Encourage children to retell or reenact stories in their own words?

☐ Engage children in dramatic play and acting out favorite stories?

☐ Find meaningful ways to introduce children to a range of writing forms and genres?

☐ Help children to write in different ways for different purposes?

PHONOLOGICAL AWARENESS

Do you . . .

- [ ] Draw children's attention to the sounds they hear in words?

- [ ] Play a variety of games that emphasize rhyming and beginning sounds?

- [ ] Read and reread stories that have predictable sound patterns?

- [ ] Provide children with time to write on their own each day?

- [ ] Sing, rhyme, and clap out the syllables of songs and chants?

- [ ] Build word walls of words with similar sound patterns?

- [ ] Use daily classroom routines to talk about words and songs?

LETTERS AND WORDS

Do you . . .

- [ ] Read alphabet books and help children identify letters?

- [ ] Write and display children's names and other words of particular interest?

- [ ] Involve children in writing activities?

- [ ] Demonstrate the writing process through shared writing activities?

- [ ] Make paper, pencils, and markers easily accessible?

- [ ] Encourage children to try to spell words out independently as they write?

- [ ] Give specific help in learning letter/sound patterns?

- [ ] Help children to learn new words?

- [ ] Help children acquire a basic sight vocabulary?

Section 3:

ENSURING CHILDREN'S READING AND WRITING SUCCESS

Informing Instruction in Reading and Writing

Making It Happen

Frequently Asked Questions

Glossary

Resources

Informing Instruction in Reading and Writing

Connie's family has been in the United States for only a year or so, and her English is quite limited. While she usually is very quiet in Ms. Smith's class, she seems to become animated during writing time. Often she draws colorful objects and then labels them with a string of letters. At first the letters she used did not correspond to the sound of the words. Several weeks ago, for example, she wrote h x m t p to mean "come to my house." Today Ms. Smith notices something new. Connie has drawn a picture of her house and written mx hws ("my house"). Ms. Smith takes down a note: "Connie is beginning to develop the alphabetic principle."

Xavier's family came to the United States from Puerto Rico, but he is fluent in English. When he turned 4, he started pointing to individual words and reading them correctly. A classroom leader, Xavier can often be found looking with friends at all sorts of print materials—even English-Spanish books. Today he tries to tackle some Spanish words, like *cielo* (sky), pronouncing it "kello." His teacher writes down this example, then records, "Xavier seems to be interested in learning words in both languages."

Christopher is new to the school setting, never having attended preschool. During classroom reading he just can't sit still—he hides under the table or climbs on the chairs until Mr. Lopez has to stop reading. His treatment of books in the classroom library is even more of a concern. He rides them like skateboards and sometimes tears them up. His teacher writes, "Christopher needs some book-handling skills and would benefit from one-to-one reading activity and reading at home with a member of his family."

Early childhood educators experience situations like these every day in their teaching. In each case, knowing what to do and how to support children's learning requires informed instructional decisionmaking *and* a plan of action. This is the heart of assessment, "the process of observing, recording, and otherwise documenting work that children do and how they do it, as a basis for a variety of educational decisions that affect the child" (NAEYC & NAECS/SDE 1992, 22).

Effective assessment makes it possible for teachers to

• monitor and document children's progress over time

• ensure that instruction is responsive and appropriately matched to what children are and are not able to do

• customize instruction to meet individual children's strengths and needs

• enable children to observe their own growth and development

• identify children who might benefit from more intensive levels of instruction, such as individual tutoring, or other interventions.

PRINCIPLES OF ASSESSMENT IN READING AND WRITING

Teaching and assessment are complementary processes; one activity informs the other. The following principles should be considered in designing an assessment program.

Assessment should support children's development and literacy learning

Good assessment helps to identify children's strengths, needs, and progress toward specific learning goals. The information gathered from this process can be used for program planning and decisionmaking to ensure that classroom instruction and activities are responsive to and appropriate for children's current level. It may also document who might benefit from special help or need more academically challenging material.

Assessment should take many different forms

Good assessment uses a variety of tools, including collections of children's work (drawings, paintings, writing), and records of conversations and interviews with children. Multiple methods ensure a more valid and reliable assessment of children's literacy progress in its many dimensions and forms. For example, a child may use a different form of writing in a play situation than he would use when writing in a journal. The core of assessment is daily observation. Watching children's ongoing life in the classroom enables teachers to capture children's performance in real activities rather than those contrived to isolate specific skills.

> **Teaching and assessment are complementary processes; one activity informs the other.**

Assessment must avoid cultural bias

Children from different cultures, linguistic groups, and backgrounds have varied experiences and styles of learning. When planning assessment, and when interpreting and reporting results to others, these factors need to be carefully considered. Some children will be further along the literacy continuum than others who may need more time, more one-to-one instruction, and more practice. At the same time, it is important to ensure that all children attain similar standards of learning and performance.

Assessment should encourage children to observe and reflect on their own learning progress

Though young children cannot be involved in every aspect of assessment, asking for their input can be a key factor in helping them learn and take ownership of their successes. Ideally, since teaching and learning are collaborative processes, children need to feel like insiders rather than outsiders, as if assessment is something that the teacher "does" to them. On the other hand, when children and teachers work and think together, assessment becomes a shared responsibility with children becoming enthusiastic team players in their own learning.

Assessment should shed light on what children are able to do as well as the areas where they need further work

Focusing on what children are able to do to help them extend what they know builds confidence and motivation for learning to read. Children are able to progress more readily in an atmosphere in which mistakes are viewed as ways to learn rather than failures to be avoided at all costs. And when teachers understand the abilities of their learners better, it becomes much easier to decide which new literacy experiences should be offered to help them develop further. This is a constructive way of looking at literacy learning for teachers and children.

ASSESSMENT PROCEDURES

Teachers today have an overwhelming array of techniques that can be used in the assessment process. Some of these instruments involve formal assessment procedures such as standardized tests. These formal measures tend to focus on comparing children's reading performance and are typically used for accountability purposes.

The primary purpose of another set of assessment methods, described as informal or authentic, is to help teachers understand what children are able to do and to provide meaningful instruction. These assessment procedures demand greater teacher knowledge and interpretation, but the depth and specificity of the information that is learned is well worth the effort.

Here are examples of some of the most common informal assessment procedures.

Anecdotal notes

Observations about children's literacy in action can provide powerful and reliable information to teachers. Ideally, teachers schedule a time every day to focus on particular children and make brief logs or anecdotal notes about the children's involvement in literacy events. Different language and literacy contexts are examined, such as one-to-one interactions, small group discussions, and large class settings, with the focus always being on what children are actually doing as they read and write. (See Figure A.)

FIGURE A: Observable Behaviors for Anecdotal Notes

PHONEMIC AWARENESS

Observable behaviors

1. Can hear and pronounce the sounds of English correctly
2. Can "stretch" a word out to hear the sounds
3. Can hear the distinctions between words in continuous speech

PHONICS: LETTER AND SOUND RELATIONSHIPS

Observable behaviors

1. Can recognize the visual form and name the letters of the alphabet
2. Can identify initial consonants in context
3. Can identify rhyming words
4. Can recognize spelling patterns and use more conventional spelling in writing
5. Can recognize some high-frequency words (list)

BOOK HANDLING SKILLS

Observable behaviors

1. Holds the book appropriately
2. "Reads" from front to back
3. Knows the difference between the pictures and the words

4. Understands the terms "beginning of" and "end of" the book
5. Understands the term "cover of the book"

CONCEPTS ABOUT PRINT

Observable behaviors

1. Points to the words and not the pictures while being read to
2. Is able to touch each word as it is read (one-to-one correspondence)
3. Knows that we read from left to right and top to bottom
4. Knows that we read a book from front to back
5. Knows the difference between a letter, a word, and a sentence

COMPREHENSION

Observable behaviors

I. Answers literal questions about text
2. Paraphrases text when asked what it was about
3. Can give the main idea of a story
4. Can answer critical questions about text
5. Asks questions when meaning is not clear

Cecil, N.L. 1999. *Striking a balance: Positive practices for early literacy.* Scottsdale, AZ: Holcomb Hathaway.

Narratives

Narratives help tell a story about a learning experience for or by children. Sometimes parts of a narrative are written at different times, but their purpose is to make more visible to others change and growth in a child's knowledge, skills, and dispositions. In many cases writings or artifacts (children's drawings) are used to provide rich examples of children's learning, helping parents and others see reading and writing as a developmental process.

Story retellings

When teachers ask children to retell a story after having read or listened to one, they gain important information about language and literacy development. Children's understandings of narrative or expository structure can be determined through an analysis of their knowledge of characters, settings, story events, and outcomes. Listening to their retellings over time helps teachers determine children's progress and understandings of basic story elements, which are essential to comprehension.

Here is a retelling of the book *Whose Mouse are You?* by Robert Krauss. The story follows a classic cat-and-mouse chase game. As a 4-year-old retells it:

This is a story about a silly mouse. Once there was a mouse that lived in a castle with a ghost. A haunted house. There was a cat in the house. And the cat chased the mouse all around the house, but he couldn't catch him. Then the mouse went to the Rocky Mountains and he got off of one of the mountains, and stood on the haunted house. And then he saw the cat. And they became friends. Then they had jello, cake, and food and had a party. And that's the end.

Writing folders

Records of children's writings at various stages, kept in writing folders, may be used for many purposes. Teachers can examine children's understanding of stories, their spelling development, and their developing concepts of print. They can also ask children about their personal reflections about any piece they have completed. These materials provide the basis for teacher/child conferences on individual needs and progress over a period of time.

Instructional conversations

Conversations with children about their favorite stories, TV programs, or activities outside school help teachers understand children's interests, motivation to learn, and self-perceptions as literacy learners. One-to-one conversations, small-group conversations, and whole-group conversations provide information about children's reasoning strategies and thinking that can be used to develop more effective learning activities.

This conversation took place after the teacher read the children the story *The Little Red Hen:*

Teacher: Why didn't the Red Hen want to share?

Anita: Because, because, the Red Hen was mad.

Teacher: Do we sometimes get mad at our friends?

Anita: Yes, course.

Teacher: When do we get mad at our friends?

Another child: When they get mad at you.

Teacher: Oh, you get mad back at each other. *(laughter)*

Anita: When they do something that you don't like.

Ensuring Children's Reading and Writing Success

Emergent storybook readings

Teachers can learn about children's concepts of print by observing and asking questions during a shared book activity or when reading one-on-one with them. Common questions, such as, What tells the story? (the picture or the print) or Where does the story begin? (directionality, moving from left to right), and instructions, "Point with your finger as I read the words," provide important information about children's understandings of print conventions.

Informal reading inventories

An invaluable tool for teachers of first-grade and beyond, the informal reading inventory (commonly referred to as *IRI*) is an individual diagnostic reading assessment designed to identify children's instructional reading and listening levels. Either commercially available or teacher designed, an IRI includes a series of graded passages (from basal reading series or leveled texts) followed by a set of comprehension questions.

Teacher: Okay. Tell me a bit more about that.

Anita: They do something that you don't like or they'll not talk to you or not share, or not be a good friend.

Teacher: So friends can get mad at each other, right?

Anita: They can not talk to you or don't share with you or nothing.

Teacher: So being a good friend means being able to share and keep talking with your friends even though you may be mad? What do you think the Red Hen might do?

Anita: Maybe let the dog and cat eat the bread after all.

The child is asked to read a graded passage aloud while the teacher carefully documents the child's deviations from the text. After the oral reading, the teacher asks a series of comprehension questions. If a child is correctly able to read approximately 90 out of 100 words and answer more than 75% of the comprehension questions, the passage is considered to be at her instructional level. Below that the passage is considered to be at her frustrational level—too difficult for the child to read with understanding.

Running records

Developed by Marie Clay, the running record is similar to the informal reading inventory but somewhat more flexible. With the running record, a child reads aloud a passage of text that is considered to be challenging or at his instructional level. In contrast to the IRI, the purpose of the running record is not so much to place the child in an instructional-leveled text, but to document the child's particular use of decoding and comprehension strategies. As the child reads each word, the teacher places a check mark on her copy of the text for every correct word, and records any errors to indicate a substitution, repetition, or mispronunciation. After the oral reading the child is asked to retell the story in his own words. Using this information, the teacher classifies the child's errors to enable her to examine the word identification strategies being used, and the child's comprehension skills, in order to make further instructional decisions.

These and other assessment strategies, when done regularly, can help teachers get to know children better—their knowledge, skills, and dispositions in learning about reading and writing. But the specific selection of assessment procedures should always be determined by the purposes of the assessment. This suggests that assessment strategies will vary according to the information being sought by teachers. For example, the table to the right shows purposes matched to types of assessment.

ORGANIZING AND REPORTING ASSESSMENT INFORMATION

Many separate pieces of information and work samples can make it hard to see the forest for the trees and get a coherent picture of children's progress toward becoming readers and writers. Therefore, it is critical to organize these materials in a way that is useful for planning instruction.

Purpose	Type of assessment
To determine a child's comprehension	Ask her to retell a story in her own words
To examine a child's phonemic awareness	Ask him to draw a picture and write about it in his own words
To evaluate a child's concepts of print	Observe how a child reads a story independently; look for where or if she points a finger at the words; see if she looks at first the left then the right page

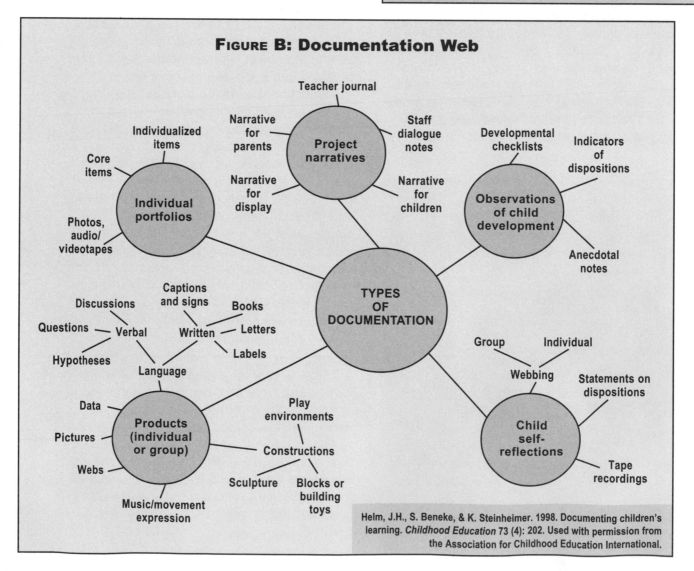

FIGURE B: Documentation Web

Helm, J.H., S. Beneke, & K. Steinheimer. 1998. Documenting children's learning. *Childhood Education* 73 (4): 202. Used with permission from the Association for Childhood Education International.

FIGURE C: Sample Profile

Summary of Literacy Growth

Child's name _____ *Age* _____ *Date* _____

Literacy   Usually / Sometimes / Never

1. Grasps/manipulates writing tools
2. Records ideas...
   using drawing for writing
   using pictures and scribble for writing
   using scribble for writing
   using letter-like forms for writing
   using letterforms randomly
   using invented spellings
   using conventional spellings
3. Writes/recognizes own name in print
4. Is aware of print permanency
5. Is aware of print orientation
6. is aware of print-meaning associations
7. Uses pictures to "read" a storybook
8. Uses pictures and print to "read" a storybook
9. Expresses story preferences
10. Recalls details from familiar stories
11. Is aware of story sequence
12. Handles books properly

Roskos, K.A., & S.B. Neuman. 1994. Of scribbles, schemas, and storybooks: Using literacy albums to document young children's literacy growth. *Young Children* 49 (2): 83. Copyright © 1994 by K.A. Roskos and S.B. Neuman. Used with permission.

Portfolios are a helpful way of organizing various examples of children's work and progress. Artists use portfolios to demonstrate their skills and achievements; teachers can use portfolios in a similar manner to portray the literacy work and progress of each student over a period of time. Portfolios typically include samples of children's writings, story retellings, interests, reading logs, and so forth, that the teacher and child have chosen.

The *documentation web* shown in Figure B highlights the multiple strategies that teachers and children themselves may use to assess and document children's progress in learning—for instance, project narratives, child self-reflections, and developmental checklists. Using a range of these strategies helps to capture the different contexts in which children learn and their various kinds of learning and development to create an integrated portrait of the child as literacy learner.

Finally, teachers can compile in a *group profile* the individual performance of each child in the class. Such a profile may be done on a single dimension or behavior or on a whole set of behaviors. (Figure C shows a sample literacy profile.) The group profile has several uses. First, it allows the teacher to get a sense of where the class as a whole is on particular skills. Compiling profiles of literacy growth, for example, helps teachers target skills in which children need extra practice, such as sequencing story events or recalling details from stories. Second, the profile enables the teacher to identify clusters of children who exhibit similar strengths and needs. Finally, the teacher can see where an individual child fits in the overall group and what areas need special attention.

HOW ASSESSMENT BENEFITS YOUNG CHILDREN

Teachers need to know as much as possible about the children in their program in order to plan activities that are useful and interesting for the group as a whole, tailor instruction to meet individual needs, and design challenging and achievable curriculum. Teachers, administrators, parents, policymakers—all of us need to keep in mind that language and literacy assessment is a means and not an end in itself. As such, it must be undertaken and conducted by responsible and informed adults for children's benefit, with the ultimate goal of assisting them to become lifelong literacy learners.

Making It Happen

One thing the president of the United States, members of Congress, state legislators, school board members, and other policymakers at all levels of government seem to have in common is that they want America's school children to achieve, especially in reading and writing. They don't agree on how to make it happen, but the shared goal is a good beginning.

In their position statement, the International Reading Association and the National Association for the Education of Young Children emphasize that achieving the goal of all children becoming independent and productive readers by the end of third grade is the shared responsibility of teachers, families, community members, and policymakers. Other sections of this book describe what teachers and parents can do; but clearly they cannot do it alone. Above all else they need more and better resources.

Providing resources to promote early literacy is where policymakers can make their greatest contribution. The complex goal of all children becoming successful readers is more likely to be attained if policymakers use their power to ensure that a fully funded infrastructure is in place and in particular that inequities in access to health care, high-quality preschool and child care programs, libraries, qualified teachers, and other necessary conditions are addressed. Such support is needed at every level—federal, state, and community. To obtain the necessary resources, teachers and parents must become literacy advocates for children and form partnerships with others who share their goals.

So, where to begin? First, we describe what needs to be done, and then we suggest the process—coalition building—that will help make it happen for all children.

WHAT NEEDS TO HAPPEN?

The IRA/NAEYC position statement identifies key policies that must be in place to provide an adequate infrastructure for achieving literacy goals. Most of these policies are set at the state or local level but can be heavily influenced by policies and funding priorities at the federal level or by public/private partnerships. Advocates need to focus the attention of decisionmakers on these key policy questions. Most of the questions are addressed to state legislators; others are addressed to boards of education. The federal government also has a role to play, especially in funding research, demonstrations, or state initiatives, as the 1999 Reading Excellence Act does, or in promoting involvement and awareness through the America READS! challenge.

Helping all children become independent, productive readers by the end of third grade is a responsibility shared by teachers, families, community members, and policymakers.

> Wherever early childhood professional development is offered, knowledge of and competence in promoting literacy need to be part of the curriculum.

KEY QUESTIONS FOR POLICYMAKERS

1. Is there a system of professional preparation and ongoing professional development in place that ensures that all teachers of young children are deeply knowledgeable, competent, and current in their profession?

Teachers can't teach what they don't know. The knowledge base that guides practice in early literacy has expanded greatly in the last decade, and yet teacher education programs at many institutions of higher education do not reflect this knowledge. In addition, many teachers—even certified teachers who are part of public school systems—do not have opportunities for ongoing professional development to keep them current in their practice. Professional development is most effective when it gives teachers opportunities to expand their knowledge and see it demonstrated in good practice, to try new approaches and reflect on their effectiveness with the support of mentors, coaches, or a peer group.

A bigger problem is the lack of a uniform professional preparation system for teachers and caregivers working in child care centers, family child care homes, and preschool programs. Wherever early childhood professional development is offered—whether in training for Child Development Associate (CDA) Credentials or at associate- or baccalaureate-degree granting institutions—knowledge of and competence in promoting literacy need to be part of the curriculum. People working with children from birth to age 5 are usually not required to have formal preservice education before employment, so professional development experiences are even more important. Connections between levels of the system too often are lacking, which impedes continuous professional development—a serious problem that state policy can and should address.

2. Are high-quality child care and preschool programs accessible and affordable for families that want or need them for their children?

Many policymakers now recognize that high-quality early childhood programs make a significant contribution to children's learning and development and their readiness for school. This recognition has resulted in increased funding for Head Start and Early Head Start and in expansion of state prekindergarten programs. Even in these publicly funded arenas, however, resources are not sufficient to adequately compensate well-qualified teachers and help them continue to grow as professionals. Moreover, these programs are not accessible even to all eligible families.

Child care, including center-based programs and family child care homes, is much more neglected as an avenue for early literacy and other key areas of learning and development. Research shows that children who attend high-quality child care programs have better language and math skills, as well as social and thinking skills, into elementary school (Peisner-Feinberg et al. 1999). Unfortunately, studies repeatedly demonstrate that only about 20% of child care centers are rated *good* or *excellent*.

Why is good child care so rare? There are many reasons, including lack of uniform standards; however, a primary reason is that because staff salaries in child care are so low (less than half of public school teachers' salaries), recruiting and retaining qualified teachers becomes impossible. And of course qualified teachers are needed to achieve goals for children's early literacy learning. Improving the quality of child care calls for significant public investment, but the payoff in school readiness and later success in reading could be substantial. Efforts such as the Child Care READS! campaign (see the box on p. 116) are underway to draw attention to this problem, but much more is needed.

3. Are classroom libraries, school libraries, and public libraries stocked with a wide variety of high-quality, diverse children's books, computer software, and other media?

One of the greatest inequities in the United States is the disproportionate access to books among different sectors of the population. Young children from middle-class and upper-middle-class families often have more books in their bedrooms than children from poorer families have in their child care programs or even their neighborhoods (Krashen 1998). And the growing importance of technology as a tool for learning creates even greater disparity in access between the haves and the have nots.

Children cannot learn to read without books, and those books must be accessible. One large-scale study of young children in child care centers in low-income communities found that providing sufficient numbers of high-quality books (five per child) and training teachers to use them resulted in significant improvements in language and literacy skills that lasted into first grade (Neuman 1996). Moreover, children need to see themselves and their life experiences reflected in the books they read or they will not be motivated to read.

Policymakers must address these inequities. It is unethical for leaders to set accountability standards and test score levels for children and teachers to meet unless at the same time they hold themselves accountable for ensuring that children have the tools and teachers have the training needed to meet those goals. For reading, books are the most basic tool and libraries are the best vehicle for ensuring access.

4. Are resources available to support parents as partners in children's literacy development?

During the early years of life, parents play the greatest role in contributing to children's language and literacy development. Yet many parents, even those who are highly motivated, do not know what to do. Other parents lack basic literacy skills themselves. Fortunately, many effective family literacy and other parenting programs now exist. Family literacy and other parent partnership programs need to be part of any comprehensive policy approach to addressing the issue of early literacy.

5. Is a regular source of health care available for every child? Do children come to child care and school healthy, well fed, and rested?

Learning to read and write is not a "natural" process; it takes attention, effort, and certainly in the primary grades it takes some hard work. Children who are hungry, tired, sick, or unable to see or hear properly because of uncorrected problems cannot achieve their potential as readers and writers. Regular health care, adequate nutrition, and rest are prerequisites for achievement, but many poor children in this country do not get them. Because it is critical to maintain high expectations for all children, we must insist that support systems be in place to make learning possible for all.

6. Are standards of learning based on research and expert opinion, including teacher experts, regarding challenging but achievable learning goals for children at various points in their development? Is there flexibility in timing regarding achievement of standards and implementation of curriculum?

Perhaps the most influential education policies of the last decade have been the standards of learning, benchmarks, or outcomes (different terms are used in different places) that now dominate local decisions about curriculum, instruction, and assessment. Such learning goals are valuable for a couple of reasons: they help communicate clearly to teachers and parents what the goals are and when they should be achieved, and they provide greater uniformity of learning experiences and curriculum within and between schools.

The possible negative consequences arise when standards are unrealistic (that is, the majority of children would be unable to achieve the standards, even with good curriculum and teaching) or when they become rigid determinants of curriculum and teaching with no allowance for individual differences in learning style, rate, or opportunity. Standards can also be easily misinterpreted; they may be set as intended minimums but in practice become the whole curriculum. We see another downside to standards when their achievement is so tightly linked to grade level and test scores that no consideration is allowed for individual variation. The goal should be to design the best possible, most important standards to guide curriculum, instruction, and assessment, but to implement them with some flexibility for individual schools and children.

7. Are class sizes in child care programs and schools small enough that teachers can give individualized attention and instruction to every child? Are primary grade classes no larger than 15 to 18 children?

Teachers simply cannot provide the kind of individualized early literacy instruction needed if there are too many children in the class. Research on reading demonstrates that no one teaching approach works for every child all the time. For instance, while

Neither social promotion nor retention is the solution for children who are behind.

much evidence exists for the value of systematic code instruction, there is no consensus about how much phonics instruction is needed, for which children, or when. Such decisions will never be resolved by research but will remain in the purview of the professional judgment of teachers. For this reason professional development, as well as small class sizes, are very important.

8. Are resources and systems in place so that children who fail to make the expected progress receive tutoring and other intensive teaching approaches rather than social promotion or retention in grade?

Policymakers often demand that reading instruction be research based, teachers be accountable, and social promotion be banned. However, these same policymakers often blithely ignore the large body of research on the ineffectiveness of retention as a strategy for improving children's achievement. Neither social promotion nor retention is the solution for children who are behind, so policymakers and administrators must commit themselves to other strategies. As the IRA/NAEYC position states, "never give up, even if later intervention is more costly and time-consuming."

9. Do teachers regularly and systematically monitor children's learning progress and then adapt curriculum and instruction based on the results? Are teachers accountable for children's continuous learning progress? Is use of standardized achievement tests postponed until fourth grade?

The almost total emphasis on achievement test scores as measures of accountability makes it very difficult to provide the individualized instruction needed for most children's reading success. Standardized tests do have an important role to play, but their impact on curriculum and teaching makes it advisable to delay their use until later grades. Using a one-size-fits-all test leads to one-size-fits-all

> Policymakers are more likely to listen when parents join administrators and teachers in calling for increased funding or higher standards for child care.

teaching, which simply does not work for reading instruction in the early grades.

HOW TO MAKE IT HAPPEN

We have described some key challenges for policymakers, but each of these challenges requires advocating for specific actions and strategies. For example, one key policy is ongoing professional development for teachers. To achieve this goal, policymakers and funders should build into new or revised legislation set-asides or funding percentages to be spent on staff training. One such example is the 1998 Head Start Reauthorization, which called for improved quality and accountability in Head Start programs, particularly in the areas of literacy and teacher qualifications. Advocates helped ensure that the legislation also included funds for staff to obtain college degrees—a step in the right direction, although the funds remain insufficient and the salary incentives need to be increased if more qualified teachers are to remain in Head Start. Similarly, provision of computers or other media designed to promote literacy should include sufficient funds to train teachers in their use.

Similar actions are needed to improve quality in child care programs. Funding for child care should be based on the true cost of providing a program that meets high standards and pays teachers salaries that are commensurate with their qualifications. Such payment would not be set at market rate, the rate most people currently pay for child care, because that rate reflects sala-

ries inadequate for staff who are qualified to promote children's literacy learning.

Boards of education and other policymakers responsible for setting standards for learning or imposing testing requirements and mandated test scores should never do so without attention to the inequity in resources among schools and districts. While it is essential to have high expectations for all children's learning, it is unfair to do so without attention to the provision of well-qualified teachers, current books and curriculum materials, adequate group sizes and teacher/child ratios, health care, and other such issues addressed earlier. This does not mean that standards should vary in different communities, but that resources and support services may need to be redistributed.

We know the kinds of action policymakers need to take, but how can we get their attention? The strategy most likely to succeed is to build a coalition of individuals and groups with differing interests but common goals; that way the policy change is less likely to be perceived as self-serving for any one group. For example, policymakers are more likely to listen when parents join administrators and teachers in calling for increased funding or higher standards for child care. Likewise, parents, teachers, community members, and business people must join librarians in calling for increased funding for libraries.

The steps in building such a coalition are illustrated in the box titled "Promoting Literacy in Early Childhood: A Call to Action," by Joan Lombardi (see p. 116), which describes a community response for promoting literacy in early childhood—the Child Care READS! campaign.

IRA and NAEYC believe that although teachers have a special responsibility in achieving the goal of all children becoming independent and productive readers and writers, it is the shared responsibility of educators, families, community members, and policymakers. If these groups do indeed share the same goal for children's literacy learning, they are ethically required to help make it happen in whatever way they can.

Promoting Literacy in Early Childhood: A Call to Action

Early childhood programs need to be supported in their efforts to expand literacy activities for young children. This can happen only if we launch communitywide efforts to link literacy to quality care in our communities and if we advocate for state policies that improve the overall quality of early childhood services across the country.

A community response

The whole community can help expand language and literacy activities for young children in child care, Head Start, preschools, and other early childhood programs. With this in mind, the Child Care READS! goals were drafted to provide programs and communities with a starting point for action.

You can play an important role in promoting literacy when you . . .

• Call a communitywide meeting to talk about the importance of literacy and ways to promote the goals of Child Care READS!

• Approach the local library to help reach out to centers and family child care providers.

• Ask local civic and business groups to lend their support to purchase books and train staff on literacy.

• Ask the local principal to set up a meeting between primary teachers and community-based early childhood teachers to help brainstorm ideas to promote literacy.

• Plan a special event to raise community awareness of the importance of promoting literacy at home and in child care. Ask your local radio and television stations to cover the event.

• Enlist the support of the religious community, senior citizen groups, and college work-study students to recruit new volunteers to read to children in early childhood programs.

• Approach your local college, resource and referral agency, and other training institutions to expand training on language and literacy using the IRA/NAEYC position statement.

• Ask the local resource and referral agency to provide information on literacy to parents, providers, pediatricians, and the business community.

• Share the research findings about literacy with policymakers and other community leaders to promote the importance of quality early childhood programs.

• Hold an Early Childhood Literacy Summit that would bring together all parts of the community and state to promote language literacy and a love of learning in young children!

Taking action for quality in your state

It is not enough to promote quality early childhood education at the program or community level. We must take steps to move from the classroom to the hearing room, from the living room to the boardroom in our efforts to improve public policies that affect young children and their families.

You can help support quality in your state when you work to . . .

• Improve the training and compensation of early childhood through investments in scholarship funds tied to salary increases or through the development of a state child care corps that would provide salary supplements for early childhood staff.

• Increase reimbursement rates tied to quality improvement and expand direct support for programs.

• Improve staff qualifications, group size, and child/staff ratio in licensing standards for the care of babies and toddlers, preschoolers, and school-age children.

• Require literacy training as a part of credentialing and licensure of all early childhood providers.

• Promote accreditation and regular monitoring of early childhood programs and family child care providers.

• Provide consumer awareness and parent education regarding the importance of quality care to child development.

• Support health consultation and health outreach in all early childhood programs and family child care homes.

• Establish benchmarks for child care quality across programs that are linked to outcomes for children.

• Expand investments in research, demonstration, and evaluation of early childhood services.

In establishing goals for your community coalition, these questions are important for each organization to answer:

• Why is your organization concerned about children acquiring literacy skills?

• What do you see as key elements in giving children a good start in reading and writing?

• What changes do you think are needed in the community (or state)?

• How much effort (time and resources) is your organization willing to contribute?

• Is your organization willing to support a range of strategies and initiatives involving a variety of service providers whose goal is to enhance children's literacy?

— *Joan Lombardi*

Frequently Asked Questions

Since the IRA and the NAEYC released their joint position statement on early literacy, teachers and others have raised a number of questions. Here are responses to some of those most frequently asked.

Is it appropriate to set the goal that every child read by the end of third grade?

Absolutely, and the IRA/NAEYC position statement supports this goal. The end of third grade is a particularly important time in schooling because at that point the expectation changes from "learning to read" to "reading to learn." Although every child is unique, each having his own rate of development, interests, and learning style, with very few exceptions all children can learn to read. However, some children need more systematic instruction, repetition, time, and practice to learn reading skills. Some need the assistance of one-on-one attention and small-group interactions. Therefore, while our goal does not change, our methods of instruction vary to meet the needs of individual children. Teachers must expect all children to master the same ambitious content and skills, while recognizing that some children progress by different methods and at different rates.

What about children who are not reading at grade level by the end of third grade? Shouldn't they be held back?

Many state boards of education now require that children pass standardized tests in reading and other subjects, usually in third grade but sometimes even earlier, before they can be promoted to the next grade. Such policies generally are intended to make the educational system more accountable for children's learning, which is a laudable goal. Unfortunately, there are two problems with this approach. One is that standardized testing may be quite inaccurate in measuring young children's progress in reading, and too much is at stake to rely on such an index. The second problem is that research tells us that retaining children in grade is counterproductive; children rarely catch up and more often fall farther behind (Shepard & Smith 1989). Nor does the answer lie in social promotion, the practice of keeping children with their age group even though they have not learned the requisite skills and content.

The IRA/NAEYC position statement calls for teacher accountability in the form of regular, ongoing assessment of children's performance during real reading tasks. It also calls for using individualized instructional strategies (as described in the previous answer) instead of retaining children or socially promoting them. All individualized strategies should be exhausted before retention is even considered. Retaining in grade should be the last resort, not the first.

My state board of education has adopted standards or benchmarks for children's learning linked to grade levels. I'm not sure they're developmentally appropriate. What should I do?

The standards movement, which swept the country in the 1990s, has had a profound effect on education. It has the positive effect of helping teachers, parents, and children know what the learning goals and expectations are. In many cases it has also raised expectations to more closely reflect what children are capable of doing. But there is a negative side to standards. Sometimes there are too many specific standards, and the curriculum becomes incoherent. Other times the standards may be too high, too low or rather trivial in nature. Standards themselves need to be developmentally appropriate—that is, challenging but achievable for most of the children in an age group, given good teaching and many enriching learning experiences.

To determine if the standards are developmentally appropriate, begin by checking the process used to develop them. As much as possible, standards should be based on what research says about children's capabilities. In cases where research is lacking or conflicting, many teachers and other experts (from different perspectives) should be consulted to review the standards.

If standards are not achievable as well as challenging, children become frustrated. Research shows that beginning readers need to experience a very high rate of success (90 to 95%) to persist at the task. So setting standards that are developmentally appropriate is essential. When teachers find problems with the standards, they should discuss these issues with other teachers and administrators and engage parents in the discussion as well. Recommended changes to standards, along with substantiating evidence, should be submitted to the appropriate parties because standards need to be periodically reviewed and revised.

We should not confuse standards or outcomes with teaching methods. For example, practitioners may look at the standard, "By the end of kindergarten children will know all the names of the letters," and begin heatedly arguing about why drilling children on letters is inappropriate. But the standard does not advocate particular teaching practices, it only states what children should know or be able to do. It is up to educators to determine the best ways to help each child reach the goal.

I've heard that many states have mandated phonics-only programs. What do we know about the effectiveness of various approaches?

There is no universal best method for teaching reading. The short answer to the question of what is most effective is "a balanced approach." But balance can mean very different things to different people. People sometimes tend to think a balanced approach means spending equal time using each approach, like balancing a scale. However, it is more a matter of integrating key elements in a seamless program. Research in the primary grades shows that children's reading achievement is highest with an instructional approach that includes both wide reading and systematic code instruction. For preschoolers programs should promote phonemic and print awareness and offer many opportunities for reading, being read to, writing, talking, and playing, as described throughout this book.

What are developmentally appropriate ways of teaching phonemic awareness in preschool?

Phonemic awareness is the ability to hear and distinguish the smallest sounds of the language. The English language uses a 26-letter alphabet to represent 44 different sounds. These sounds make up all the words we speak and write. It's quite a wonderful and efficient system! Research shows that children who are adept at phonemic awareness in kindergarten are much more likely to become successful readers. Even more striking is the extent to which very low phonemic awareness is correlated with difficulty in learning to read. Without this important skill, the learning of letter/sound relationships (phonics) does not make sense.

So, we know that phonemic awareness is important, but how do we foster its development? Activities that involve playing with language—singing, doing fingerplays, playing rhyming games, listening to poems, clapping out the syllables of names or words, and reading books such as those by

Dr. Seuss—need to be a regular part of the preschool day for all children. Teachers need to be intentional about planning such experiences and choosing books, songs, and materials that promote phonemic awareness. They also need to keep track of children's progress in this ritual area.

At the same time, we should remember that more goes into learning words than just phonemic awareness. It is a key skill but by no means the only language skill that is critical for success in reading. On pages 28-95, of this book we identify seven other dimensions important to children's literacy learning, such as building background knowledge and language development.

What kind of phonics instruction is best?

Starting in kindergarten the goal of phonics instruction is to provide children with a method for figuring out unfamiliar words. Learning how to translate spellings to speech sounds is important for independent word recognition. The best way to help children, then, is to draw their attention to common word families (-at, -ot, -it) and a few basic rules that they may encounter often (consonant-vowel-consonant, like c-a-t; silent e rule, such as b-a-k-e). Spending some time each day on the spelling/sound patterns is a good use of children's instructional time.

Phonics instruction by itself is not enough, however. Skillful reading requires practice in seeing and understanding decodable words in real reading situations. The ideal phonics instruction helps children develop skills that they soon use automatically. Slow, laborious reading, where children try to sound out everything, should be avoided. Rather, phonics instruction works best when it is part of a reading program that puts these skills in practice in reading and writing for meaningful purposes.

How do you improve the literacy skills of young children who haven't had many literacy learning experiences before they come to school?

Some educators suggest that children far behind their peers need drill-and-practice activities, including isolated letter or phonics instruction at the most rudimentary level. But for most of these children, the real basics are extending their language and vocabulary, increasing their awareness of print, and introducing them to the pleasures and purposes of reading and writing. Trying to learn letter/sound connections, for example, without understanding the literacy act is confusing and too abstract for children. We need to begin with the large picture—the purposes of reading and writing—and show children how literacy functions in daily activities. Children then become interested in finding out how reading and writing work, how letters and sounds come together to form words, and how these words tell a story. Of critical importance too are developing children's oral language and providing interesting curriculum studies that broaden children's background knowledge—all key to reading comprehension.

I have a group of four- and five-year-olds who among them have five different home languages. What do I do about children whose home language is other than standard English?

To begin with, we should recognize that children with limited English are not necessarily children with little language. Teachers can then build on children's home language and culture. This is an area where relationships with families are essential. When teachers do not speak the child's language, they cannot assess the child's competence. They need information from families, and they need to work with family members to help them support their children's literacy development in the home language as much as possible. Children who begin school or preschool with a native language other than standard English need a rich diet of language experiences that builds on the knowledge of their first language and enables them to learn a second language. Research confirms that reading aloud to children in small groups is one of the best ways to ensure a rich resource of language. Children learn new words by listening to stories and by talking to others about them.

Teachers need to consider a number of supports for language learning. Early in their language acquisition, children have difficulty grasping meaning from listening to a stream of speech alone. In conversation, gestures, facial expressions, and visual aids (pointing to objects, showing pictures) help to verify and validate children's comprehension. Organizing the classroom environment with interesting materials and opportunities for collaborative hands-on experiences helps children with limited English feel like they are members of the classroom community. (For more strategies for helping English-language learners, see p. 55).

It is impossible to learn to read in a language that you do not speak. Children who are not proficient in English should be given opportunity and time to become proficient in the oral language before formal reading instruction begins. Children can, however, be acquiring early literacy skills in their home language (for example, phonemic and print awareness) while simultaneously learning English. If children learn to read in another alphabetic language, the skills transfer to help them achieve proficiency in English.

Children who speak a dialect of English will be assisted in learning to read if teachers are familiar with the dialect. Teachers then can help children recognize which sounds vary between the dialect and the standard English expected in school and in the larger society.

Is invented spelling good or bad for children?

Invented spelling has been the victim of very bad press in the United States. Research actually shows that using temporary invented spelling, also called *developmental* or *phonetic spelling,* contributes to children's success as readers and writers. It certainly draws their attention to the sounds of letters and parts of words. It also helps them advance as writers because they are not limited to expressing themselves in words they already know how to spell. The IRA/NAEYC position statement addresses such developmental spelling and points out that by second grade, children should be moving toward conventional spelling and editing their written products so that their own spellings are used only in drafts. Actually, many adults use invented spelling daily. When adults using word processing software get to a word they can't spell, they approximate the spelling so they can keep moving and later use a spell checking program to correct it! (For more on developmental spellings, see p. 86.)

With the current emphasis on literacy in preschool and kindergarten, many teachers are using curriculums that focus on one letter at a time. Is "letter of the week" a good way to teach early literacy?

Letters of the alphabet are often confusing for young children. Some of the letters look alike, such as *p* and *q* and *m* and *n.* And letters themselves are abstract—they are symbols that stand for something else, not the real object. No matter how well the alphabet is taught, it may be difficult for children to grasp and make sense of this new symbol system when only one letter is presented at a time. Furthermore, teaching one letter a week takes almost the whole school year to get through the alphabet, by which time adults may be disappointed to find that children have forgotten the first letters in the sequence.

Perhaps more distressing, the letter of the week often becomes the primary source of the preschool or kindergarten curriculum, which does not promote intellectually engaging learning experiences or powerful conceptual development. Learning the alphabet is necessary, but it should be only one outcome of a strong curriculum that addresses all areas of children's development and learning.

Children learn alphabet letters most readily when the letters appear in meaningful settings. Picture displays with the words carefully printed next to them help children associate letters with something memorable. Alphabet puzzles, imprinting in play dough, and magnetic letters help children learn the letters by comparing similarities and differences in their sizes and shapes. Writing children's names (or calling out the letters as the child writes them) helps children learn and identify letters more efficiently and effectively. (For more on letter learning, see pp. 88–95.)

Is it wrong to use basal readers to teach reading?

No. Basal readers can be useful tools if used appropriately. As mentioned throughout this book, effective instruction builds on prior knowledge and skills. Basal readers are commercial packages of materials that include graded series of texts for kindergarten through grade six along with instructional manuals for teachers, detailed lesson plans, and activities and manipulatives for children. To the extent that the programs provide opportunities for individualization and a rationale for activities, including tips and tools for teaching skills, they can be of value for improving children's performances in reading.

The problem comes with overreliance on the basal readers, allowing them to become the total reading program. A more effective strategy is to select carefully from the menu of activities these program offer; balance skills, strategies, and opportunities for pleasurable reading; and ensure that all children have daily opportunities for independent reading of trade books.

Is seatwork bad for children?

It depends on several conditions, especially the age of the child and the task required. For preschoolers and younger, time required in seats should be limited. However, when children self-select to write or do a puzzle or some other seated activity, they may stay seated for an extended period of time. There is nothing inherently wrong with seatwork for primary-grade children. In addition to exercising valuable skills, many children enjoy the sense of getting something done. Well-devised seatwork can provide opportunities for children in the primary grades to practice the knowledge and skills they need the most.

Unfortunately though, in many cases seatwork is a waste of time. Children may not profit because the work is too hard, and thereby perpetuates mistakes and misinforma-

tion, or it is too easy and does not make good use of their minds and energies. The best recommendation then is to give seatwork only if and when children can genuinely profit from it. But remember, time spent on seatwork is time not spent on reading.

Can you describe the term scaffolding in teaching?

Scaffolding is a teaching strategy in which the adult provides temporary assistance to a child working on a task that at that point in time he cannot manage to do on his own. A scaffold is a temporary structure that helps a person reach or do something that would otherwise be beyond reach. In teaching a child to write his name the first time, for instance, the teacher does more than just write the letters and expect the child to copy them. Instead, she builds on what the child can do on his own with what he can do with assistance, as in this exchange: "Your name is Brian. How do you make a *B*?" "I draw a straight line, but I can't make the rest." "I'll show you. It's like two half circles on a stick."

Our school is adopting a well-known reform program. What are the most effective early reading-intervention programs?

Several of the best known reading-intervention programs share certain features yet differ substantially in approach. Decisions about adopting any such program should carefully consider evaluation evidence, analyze cost and benefits, and assess the match between the program's approach or philosophy and that of the school. Two of the most well known and extensively researched early-intervention programs to date are Reading Recovery, a tutorial reading program designed by Marie Clay, and Success for All, a schoolwide program developed by Robert Slavin. These programs use quite different approaches but share some common features that may account for their benefits.

The Reading Recovery program uses one-on-one tutoring for first graders whose progress in reading is not on course. Exten-

Ensuring Children's Reading and Writing Success

sively trained tutors work daily with individual children in 1½-hour blocks for 60 sessions. Each lesson involves readings of new and familiar books, running records to assess reading fluency, letter/sound exercises, and writing activities. Teachers typically work with four children a day or 8 to 11 children per year. Although in recent years there has been increasing controversy as to whether the benefits of Reading Recovery are sustained over time, considerable evidence indicates that with effective classroom instruction the gains made in the remedial part of the program are maintained.

Success for All is a schoolwide intervention program for children in kindergarten through third grade who are at risk for early reading failure. Key features include individualized tutoring, cooperative learning, smaller teacher-student ratios for reading, regrouping across grade levels to establish homogeneous groups, assessments, and specially designed decodable basal readers. Like Reading Recovery, Success for All has had its share of controversy. Its critics cite the prescriptiveness of the approach and the limited opportunity to adapt the material to children's interests. On the other hand, some teachers value the clarity and direction of the program. There is also some controversy over its effectiveness; however, research is generally positive with over half of the more than 200 sites showing significant gains in reading compared to other schools not in the program.

These and other reading intervention programs share a number of elements that any school wishing to improve children's performances in reading should take into consideration. Certain key elements are congruent with the IRA/NAEYC policy recommendations. They include rejection of retention in favor of intervention; individualized instruction through tutoring and smaller groupings; smaller class sizes and better teacher-child ratios; well-trained teachers; and a balanced approach to reading instruction using systematic code instruction and meaningful connected reading.

I teach kindergarten in a poor, urban school district, and I have a friend who teaches at an elite private school. We both get pressure from parents to teach reading and writing in ways and at ages we don't think are appropriate. What should we do?

The most important thing to do is establish common ground with parents. It is likely that you share a common goal—that children become successful readers and writers. Once that shared priority is established, then much communication must follow about how you are both working to achieve that goal. Negotiation may also be required. You may need to be more explicit in some of your instruction or the parents may need to learn about the value of strategies such as developmental spelling and dramatic play in promoting literacy. Once you've established relationships with parents, both you and they are more likely to learn and change.

Be sure to thoughtfully reflect on your teaching practices and expectations for children and make sure that what you are doing is in keeping with the current knowledge about how and when children learn to read and write. Use this book and the other resources listed in the book to become familiar with that knowledge. Pay special attention to the developmental continuum in the first section (pp. 20–23), which describes appropriate expectations, and to the section Readers and Writers in the Making, which describes and illustrates good practice. Parents and others who enter your classroom should see so much evidence of children's engagement in literacy activities in the display of their products that they need never question how effectively you teach reading and writing. Be sure to document each child's progress in reading and writing development and regularly communicate with her parents about it. For instance, explain the stages of writing and show the child's samples collected over time that demonstrate her learning.

GLOSSARY

Alphabetic principle: The understanding that there is a systematic relationship between letters and sounds. For example, the word *dog* contains three letters and three corresponding sounds.

Big Book: An oversize book, usually a picture book, used by the teacher for reading to a group; its large size allows children to follow the print and attend to words, letters, and sounds.

Comprehension monitoring: The ability of children to examine their understanding of what they are reading when they are reading.

Constructivism: A theory of knowledge suggesting that children are active learners who organize new information and relate it to their prior learning.

Decodable text: Beginner-oriented books that contain words that are phonetically regular, such as, "That Sam I am."

Decode: The ability to translate the alphabet letters into recognizable sounds (the letter *f* makes the /F/ sound).

Developmental (invented) spelling: Spellings that result from a beginning writer's initial attempts to associate sounds with letters. As children advance in literacy, their spelling becomes increasingly characterized by more complete understandings about the organizational patterns of words. Spelling develops from prephonemic to conventional spelling over time and with good instruction.

Dialect: A language variation; a culturally-based speech pattern that varies from the standard form used in written works.

Direct instruction: A structured, systematic lesson focusing on a specific skill.

Directionality: The concept that English print is read from left to write, top to bottom, and from the left page to the right page.

Emergent literacy: The view that literacy learning begins at birth and is encouraged through participation with adults in meaningful activities; these literacy behaviors change and eventually become conventional over time.

Emergent reading: A child's pretense of reading before he is able to read fluently and conventionally. Shows the child's interest and motivation in learning to read.

Environmental print: Print that is encountered outside of books and that is a pervasive part of everyday living.

Explicit instruction: A teacher-directed strategy that emphasizes the teaching of a specific task and the steps needed to master it.

Expository text: An informational book.

Expressive language: Children's use and knowledge of words in spoken language.

Family literacy: The different ways in which family members initiate and use literacy in their daily lives. Family literacy programs generally emphasize adult literacy skills, early reading activities, parent-child activity time, and parenting skills.

Fluency: The ability to identify letters and words automatically.

Functional print: Print for a purpose, such as informational signs, directions, lists, and messages.

Grapheme: A letter that represents a sound.

Informal assessment: A nonstandardized measurement by which a teacher gauges what a child is able to do in various areas of literacy. Informal assessment helps teachers tailor lessons to meet children's individual needs.

Interactive writing: The process in which the teacher takes down a child's dictation, verbally stretching each word so that the child can distinguish sounds and letters. Also known as shared writing.

Journals: Daily writing books that children use to record life events and stories of their choosing. For early literacy learners, journal writing is often accompanied by illustrations and developmental spellings.

K-W-L: A strategy that enhances children's comprehension by assessing "what children Know, what they Want to know, and what they Learned" before and after reading.

Letter knowledge: The ability to identify the letters of the alphabet.

Matthew effect: The phenomenon that suggests that skilled decoders get better at reading while poor decoders tend to fall further behind.

Morning message: An instructional method in which the teacher writes on a chart a meaningful message about an event or an interesting question, followed by discussion of skills and concepts of print.

Onset: All the sounds of a word that come before the first vowel, for example, bl- and b- before -ank.

Phoneme: The smallest units of sound that combine to form syllables and words (for example, b-i-g, three phonemes).

Phonemic awareness: The ability to recognize spoken words as a sequence of sounds.

Phonemic blending: Blending individual sounds to make a word, for instance, t-o-p to *top*.

Phonemic segmentation: The process of separating sounds within a word, for example, top to t-o-p.

Phonics: The relation between letters and sounds in written words or an instructional method that teaches children these connections.

Phonological awareness: The whole spectrum from primitive awareness of speech sounds and rhythms to rhyme awareness and sound similarities and, at the highest level, awareness of syllables or phonemes.

Portfolio: Much like an artist's folio, a portfolio serves to collect evidence of the child's developing literacy understandings. A portfolio might include interest inventories, samples of the child's writing, and retellings of favorite stories.

Predictable books: Books that use repetitive lines and familiar patterns that make it possible for listeners or readers to know or guess what is coming next, such as, "Brown bear, brown bear, what do you see?"

Primary language: The first language a child learns to speak, also known as their *home language*.

Receptive language: Children's listening vocabulary and knowledge of spoken words.

Repeated reading: Rereading a book to enable children to become familiar with recurring phrases and other predictable language, gain a better understanding of the story, and acquire vocabulary and concepts they might not grasp on one reading.

Retelling: A child's retelling of a story, which helps the teacher to examine her comprehension and use of language.

Rime: The first vowel in a word and all the sounds that follow, for example, -at in *that*.

Running record: A procedure for examining children's oral reading, noting their strengths and weaknesses when using various reading strategies.

Scaffolding: Appropriate adult mediation to help children accomplish more difficult tasks than they could normally do on their own.

Shared reading: A technique in which the teacher reads aloud from a Big Book, while children follow along using individual copies of the same book.

Sight vocabulary: Words that are recognized automatically, without the reader having to sound them out.

Standardized test: A testing instrument with validity and reliability from which scores are interpreted against a set of norms, such as state, national, or international norms.

Syllable: A unit of spoken language (e.g., rid-dle, two syllables).

Tracking: Showing an understanding of the correspondence of spoken and written words by finger-pointing.

Vocabulary: The words of which one has listening and speaking knowledge.

Whole language: A philosophy of teaching literacy that includes the use of trade books, with the concurrent instruction in reading, writing, and oral language, and focuses on meaningful, functional, and cooperative learning.

Word wall: A chart (or charts) listing important vocabulary which can be referred to during word study activities.

Wordless books: Picture storybooks containing no words, used to enhance storytelling and language skills.

REFERENCES
AND RESOURCES

REFERENCES

Burns, M.S., P. Griffin, & C. Snow, eds. 1999. *Starting out right: A guide to promoting children's reading success.* Washington, DC: National Academy Press.

Davidson, J. 1996. *Emergent literacy and dramatic play in early education.* Albany, NY: Delmar.

Hall, N., & A. Robinson. 1995. *Exploring writing and play in the early years.* London: Fulton.

Krashen, S. 1998. Bridging inequity with books. *Educational Leadership:* 18–22.

NAEYC & National Association of Early Childhood Specialists in State Departments of Education (NAECS/SDE). 1992. Position statement on guidelines for appropriate curriculum content and assessment in programs serving children ages 3 through 8. [Adopted 1990.] In *Reaching potentials: Appropriate curriculum and assessment for young children, Volume 1*, eds. S. Bredekamp & T. Rosegrant. Washington, DC: NAEYC.

Neuman, S.B. 1996. Children engaging in storybook reading: The influence of access to print resources, opportunity, and parental interaction. *Early Childhood Research Quarterly* 11: 495–514.

Peisner-Feinberg, E.S., M.R. Burchinal, R.M. Clifford, M.L. Culkin, C. Howes, S.L. Kagan, N. Yazejian, P. Byler, & J. Rustici. 1999. *The children of the Cost, Quality, and Outcomes Study go to school. Technical report.* Chapel Hill: University of North Carolina, Frank Porter Graham Child Development Center.

Schickedanz, J.A. 1999. *Much more than the ABCs: The early stages of reading and writing.* Washington, DC: NAEYC.

Shepard, L., & M.L. Smith. 1989. *Flunking grades: Research and policies on retention.* Bristol, PA: Taylor & Francis.

ADDITIONAL RESOURCES

Adams, M.J., B. Foorman, I. Lundberg, & T. Beeler. 1998. Phonemic awareness in young children: A classroom curriculum. Baltimore, MD: Brookes.

Areglado, N., & M. Dill, 1998. *Let's write: A practical guide to teaching writing in the early grades.* New York: Scholastic.

Armington, D. 1997. *The living classroom: Writing, reading, and beyond.* Washington, DC: NAEYC.

Au, K. 1993. *Literacy instruction in multicultural settings.* Fort Worth, TX: Harcourt Brace.

Au, K.H., J.H. Carroll, & J.A. Scheu. 1997. *Balanced literacy instruction: A teacher's resource book.* Norwood, MA: Christopher-Gordon.

Barclay, K., C. Benelli, & A. Curtis. 1995. Literacy begins at birth: What caregivers can learn from parents of children who read early. *Young Children* 50 (4): 24–28.

Beach, S.A. 1996. Research in Review. "I can read my own story!" Becoming literate in the primary grades. *Young Children* 52 (1): 22–27.

Bean, W., & L.C. Bouffler. 1997. *Read, write, spell.* York, ME: Stenhouse.

Braunger, J., & J.P. Lewis. 1997. *Building a knowledge base in reading.* Newark, DE: International Reading Association.

Bredekamp, S., & C. Copple, eds. 1997. *Developmentally appropriate practice in early childhood programs, revised edition.* Washington, DC: NAEYC.

Bridges, L. 1997. *Writing.* York, ME: Stenhouse.

Brock, D.R., & E. Dodd. 1994. A family lending library: Promoting early literacy development. *Young Children* 49 (3): 16–21.

Cary, S. 1997. *Second language learners.* York, ME: Stenhouse.

Chambers, A. 1996. *The reading environment: How adults help children enjoy books.* York, ME: Stenhouse.

Chambers, A. 1996. *Tell me.* York, ME: Stenhouse.

Christie, J., B. Enz, & C. Vukelich. 1997. *Teaching language and literacy: Preschool through the elementary grades.* Boston, MA: Addison-Wesley.

Clay, M. 1993. *What did I write? Beginning writing behavior.* Portsmouth, NH: Heinemann.

Collins, J.L. 1998. *Strategies for struggling writers.* New York: Guilford.

Conlon, A. 1992. Giving Mrs. Jones a hand: Making group storytime more pleasurable and meaningful for young children. *Young Children* 47 (3): 14–18.

Cramer, R.L. 1998. *The spelling connection: Integrating reading, writing, and spelling instruction.* New York: Guilford.

Cunningham, P. 1991. Research directions: Multimethod, multilevel literacy instruction in first grade. *Language Arts* 68: 578–84.

Cunningham, P. 1995. *Phonics they use: Words for reading and writing.* NY: HarperCollins.

Cunningham, P., & R. Allington. 1999. *Classrooms that work: They can all read and write.* NY: Longman.

Depree, H., & S. Iversen. 1994. *Early literacy in the class-room: A new standard for young readers.* Bothell, WA: Wright Group.

Dickinson, D., ed. 1994. *Bridges to literacy: Children, families, and schools.* Cambridge, MA: Blackwell.

Dorn, L., C. French, & T. Jones. 1998. *Apprenticeship in literacy: Transitions across reading and writing.* York, ME: Stenhouse.

Duffy, G., & L. Roehler. 1987. Teaching reading skills as strategies. *The Reading Teacher* 39: 414–18.

Dyson, A.H. 1993. *Social worlds of children learning to write in an urban primary school.* NY: Teachers College Press.

Eeds, M., & D. Wells. 1989. Grand conversations: An exploration of meaning construction in literature study groups. *Research in the Teaching of English* 23: 4–29.

Elley, W. 1991. Acquiring literacy in a second language: The effect of book-based programs. *Language Learning* 41: 375–411.

Elster, C.A. 1994. I guess they do listen: Young children's emergent readings after adult read-alouds. *Young Children* 49 (3): 26–31.

Entwisle, D., K. Alexander, & L.S. Olson. 1997. *Children, schools, and inequality.* Boulder, CO: Westview.

Ericson, L., & M.F. Juliebo. 1998. *The phonological aware-ness handbook for kindergarten and primary teachers.* Newark, DE: International Reading Association.

Feagans, L., & D.C. Farran, eds. 1982. *The language of children reared in poverty: Implications for evaluation and intervention.* New York: Academic.

Ferreiro, E., & A. Teberosky. 1982. *Literacy before schooling.* Portsmouth, NH: Heinemann.

Fisher, B. 1991. *Joyful learning: A whole language kindergar-ten.* Portsmouth, NH: Heinemann.

Fitzgerald, J. 1993. Literacy and students who are learning English as a second language. *The Reading Teacher* 46: 638–47.

Fountas, I., & G.S. Pinnell. 1995. *Guided reading: Good first teaching for all children.* Portsmouth, NH: Heinemann.

Fraser, J., & D. Skolnick. 1994. *On their way: Celebrating second-graders as they read and write.* Portsmouth, NH: Heinemann.

Freeman, D., & Y. Freeman. 1993. Strategies for promoting the primary languages of all students. *The Reading Teacher* 46: 552–58.

Friedberg, J. 1989. Food for Thought. Helping today's toddlers become tomorrow's readers: A pilot parent participation project offered through a Pittsburgh health agency. *Young Children* 44 (2): 13–16.

Gable, S. 1999. Promote children's literacy with poetry. *Young Children* 54 (5): 12–15.

Gambrell, L., L.M. Morrow, S.B. Neuman, & M. Pressley, eds. 1999. *Best practices in literacy instruction.* New York: Guilford.

Glazer, S.M. 1998. *Assessment is instruction: Reading, writing, spelling, and phonics for ALL learners.* Norwood, MA: Christopher-Gordon.

Goldenberg, C. 1992/93. Instructional conversations: Promoting comprehension through discussion. *The Reading Teacher* 46: 316–26.

Greenberg, P. 1998. Some thoughts about phonics, feelings, Don Quixote, diversity, and democracy: Teaching young children to read, write, and spell, Part 1. *Young Children* 53 (4): 72–83.

Greenberg, P. 1998. Thinking about goals for grownups while we teach writing, reading, and spelling (and a few thoughts about the "J" word). *Young Children* 53 (6): 31–42.

Greenberg, P. 1998. Warmly and calmly teaching young children to read, write, and spell: Thoughts about the first four of twelve well-known principles, Part 2. *Young Children* 53 (5): 68–82.

Gross, A.L., & L.W. Ortiz. 1994. Using children's literature to facilitate inclusion in kindergarten and the primary grades. *Young Children* 49 (3): 32–35.

Gunning, T.C. 1998. *Best books for beginning readers.* Needham Heights, MA: Allyn & Bacon.

Hannon, P. 1995. *Literacy, home, and school: Research and practice in teaching literacy with parents.* London: Falmer.

Hannon, P. 1996. School is too late: Preschool work with parents. In *Family involvement in literacy: Effective partnerships in education,* eds. S. Wolfendale & K. Topping, 3–74. London: Cassell.

Hart, B., & T. Risley. 1995. *Meaningful differences in the everyday experience of young American children.* Balti-more, MD: Brookes.

Henriques, M.E. 1997. Increasing literacy among kindergartners through cross-age training. *Young Children* 52 (4): 42–47.

Hiebert, E.H., & T.E. Raphael. 1998. *Early literacy instruction.* Fort Worth, TX: Harcourt Brace.

Ingraham, P. 1997. Creating and managing learning centers: A thematic approach. Peterborough, NH: Crystal Springs.

International Reading Association (IRA). 1998. *Phonemic awareness and the teaching of reading: A position statement from the Board of Directors of the International Reading Association.* Newark, DE: Author.

Kozol, J. 1992. *Savage inequalities: Children in America's schools.* New York: HarperCollins.

Kupetz, B.N., & E.J. Green. 1997. Sharing books with infants and toddlers: Facing the challenges. *Young Children* 52 (2): 22–27.

Manning, M., G. Manning, & C. Kamii. 1988. Early phonics instruction: Its effect on literacy development. *Young Children* 44 (1): 4–8.

McGee, L., & D. Richgels. 1996. *Literacy's beginnings: Supporting young readers and writers.* 2d ed. Boston: Allyn & Bacon.

McGill-Franzen, A. 1992. Early literacy: What does "developmentally appropriate" mean? *The Reading Teacher* 46: 56–57.

McGill-Franzen, A. 1993. "I could read the words!" Selecting good books for inexperienced readers. *The Reading Teacher* 46: 424–26.

McGill-Franzen, A., & C. Lanford. 1994. Exposing the edge of the preschool curriculum: Teachers' talk about text and children's literary understandings. *Language Arts* 71: 264–73.

Moats, L. 1998. Teaching decoding. *American Educator* 22 (Spring/Summer): 42–49, 95–96.

Morrow, L.M. 1997. *The literacy center: Contexts for reading and writing.* York, ME: Stenhouse.

Morrow, L.M. 1997. *Literacy development in the early years: Helping children read and write.* New York: Allyn & Bacon.

Morrow, L.M., D. Strickland, & D.G. Woo. 1998. *Literacy instruction in half- and whole-day kindergarten: Research to practice.* Newark, DE: International Reading Association.

NAEYC & International Reading Association (IRA). 1998. *Raising a reader, raising a writer: How parents can help.* Brochure. Washington, DC: NAEYC.

Neuman, S.B. 1995. Reading together: A community-supported parent tutoring program. *The Reading Teacher* 49: 120–29.

Neuman, S.B., B.J. Caperelli, & C. Kee. 1998. Literacy learning, a family matter. *The Reading Teacher* 52: 244–53.

Neuman, S.B., & K. Roskos. 1993. Language and literacy learning in the early years. Fort Worth, TX: Harcourt Brace.

Neuman, S.B., & K. Roskos. 1994. Bridging home and school with a culturally responsive approach. *Childhood Education* 70: 210–14.

Neuman, S.B., & K. Roskos, eds. 1998. *Children achieving: Best practices in early literacy.* Newark, DE: International Reading Association.

Notari-Syverson, A., R. O'Connor, & P. Vadasy. 1998. *Ladders to literacy: A preschool activity book.* Baltimore, MD: Brookes.

Novick, R. 1998. *Learning to read and write: A place to start.* Portland, OR: Northwest Regional Education Laboratory.

Ollila, L.O., & M. Mayfield, eds. 1992. *Emerging literacy: Preschool, kindergarten, and primary grades.* Boston: Allyn & Bacon.

Ortiz, R., S. Stile, & C. Brown. 1999. Early literacy activities of fathers: Reading and writing and young children. *Young Children* 54 (5): 16–18.

Purcell-Gates, V. 1995. *Other people's words: The cycle of low literacy.* Cambridge, MA: Harvard University Press.

Quintero, E., & M.C. Velarde. 1990. Intergenerational literacy: A developmental, bilingual approach. *Young Children* 45 (4): 10–15.

Raines, S.C., & R.J. Canady. 1992. Story stretchers for the primary grades: Activities to expand children's favorite books. Mt. Rainer, MD: Gryphon House.

Rice, M.L., K.A. Wilcox, & B. Bunce. 1995. *Building a language-focused curriculum for the preschool classroom, Volume 1. A foundation for lifelong communication.* Baltimore, MD: Brookes.

Riley, J. 1996. *The teaching of reading.* London: Paul Chapman.

Roskos, K. 1988. Literacy at work in play. *The Reading Teacher* 41: 562–67.

Roskos, K., & S.B. Neuman. 1994. Of scribbles, schemas, and storybooks: Using literacy albums to document young children's growth. *Young Children* 49 (2): 83.

Roskos, K., C. Vukelich, J. Christie, B. Enz, & S.B. Neuman. 1995. *Linking literacy and play.* Videotape. Newark, DE: International Reading Association.

Rowley, R. 1992. Caregiver's Corner. Reading buddies. *Young Children* 47 (2): 55.

Shanahan, T., & S.B. Neuman. 1997. Literacy research that makes a difference. *Reading Research Quarterly* 32: 202–10.

Smith, T. 1980. Parents and Preschool. Ypsilanti, MI: High/Scope Press.

Snow, C.E., M.S. Burns, & P. Griffin, eds. 1998. *Preventing reading difficulties in young children: Committee on the Prevention of Reading Difficulties in Young Children, Commission on Behavioral and Social Sciences and Education, National Research Council.* Washington, DC: National Academy Press.

Spangenberg-Urbschat, K., & R. Pritchard. 1994. Kids come in all languages: Reading instruction for ESL students. Newark, DE: International Reading Association.

Stanovich, K.E. 1986. Matthew effects in reading: Some consequences of individual differences in the acquisition of literacy. *Reading Research Quarterly* 21: 360–406.

Strickland, D. 1994. Educating African American learners at risk: Finding a better way. *Language Arts* 71: 328–36.

Strickland, D. 1995. Reinventing our literacy programs: Books, basics, balance. *The Reading Teacher* 48: 294–303.

Strickland, D. 1998. *Teaching phonics today: A primer for educators.* Newark, DE: International Reading Association.

Teale, W.H., & M.G. Martinez. 1988. Getting on the right road to reading: Bringing books and young children together in the classroom. *Young Children* 44 (1): 10–15.

Teale, W.H., & E. Sulzby. 1989. Emergent literacy: New perspectives. In *Emerging literacy: Young children learn to read and write,* eds. D. Strickland & L.M. Morrow, 1–15. Newark, DE: International Reading Association.

Thompson, G.B., & Nicholson, T. 1998. *Learning to Read: Beyond Phonics and Whole Language.* Newark, DE: International Reading Association.

Throne, J. 1988. Becoming a kindergarten of readers? *Young Children* 43 (6): 10–16.

Trachtenburg, P., & A. Ferruggia. 1989. Big books from little voices: Reaching high risk beginning readers. *Reading Teacher* 41: 284–89.

U.S. Department of Education America Reads Challenge. 1997. Ready*Set*Read for caregivers.

Valdes, G. 1996. Con respeto: *Bridging the distances between culturally diverse families and schools: An ethnographic portrait.* New York: Teachers College Press.

Valencia, S. 1990. A portfolio approach to classroom reading assessment: The whys, whats, and hows. *The Reading Teacher* 42: 338–40.

VanSciver, J., & L. Fleetwood. 1997. Heading off first-grade retention. *Young Children* 52 (7): 16–18.

Walker-Dalhouse, D. 1993. Beginning reading and the African American child at risk. *Young Children* 49 (1): 24–28.

Waring-Chaffee, M.B. 1994. RDRNT...HRIKM. (Ready or not here I come): Investigations in children's emergence as readers and writers. *Young Children* 49 (6): 52–55.

Whitehurst, G., D. Arnold, J. Epstein, A. Angell, M. Smith, & J. Fischel. 1994. A picture book reading intervention in day care and home for children from low-income families. *Developmental Psychology* 30: 679–89.

Williams, R.P., & J.K. Davis. 1994. Lead sprightly into literacy. *Young Children* 49 (4): 37–41.

Wolter, W.L. 1992. Whole group story reading? *Young Children* 48 (1): 72–75.

NAEYC is . . .

an organization of more than 101,000 members founded in 1926 and committed to fostering the growth and development of children from birth through age 8. Membership is open to all who share a desire to serve and act on behalf of the needs and rights of young children.

NAEYC provides . . .

educational services and resources to adults and programs working with and for children, including

• **Young Children,** the peer-reviewed journal for early childhood educators

• **Books, posters, brochures, and videos** to expand your knowledge and commitment to and support your work with young children and families, including topics on infants, curriculum, research, discipline, teacher education, and parent involvement

• An **Annual Conference** that brings people together from all over the United States and other countries to share their expertise and advocate on behalf of children and families

• **Week of the Young Child** celebrations sponsored by more than 400 NAEYC Affiliate Groups to call public attention to the critical significance of the child's early years

• **Insurance plans** for members and programs

• **Public affairs** information and access to information through NAEYC resources and communication systems for conducting knowledgeable advocacy efforts at all levels of government and through the media

• **A voluntary accreditation system** for high-quality programs for children through the National Academy of Early Childhood Programs

• **Resources and services** through the National Institute for Early Childhood Professional Development, working to improve the quality and consistency of early childhood preparation and professional development opportunities

• **Young Children International** to promote international communication and information exchanges

National Association for the Education of Young Children
1509 16th Street, NW, Washington, DC 20036 • 202-232-8777 or 800-424-2460
• Website: www.naeyc.org